D1544302

YALE STUDIES IN ENGLISH

ALBERT S. COOK, Editor

XVI

THE TRANSLATIONS OF BEOWULF

A CRITICAL BIBLIOGRAPHY

BY

CHAUNCEY B. TINKER

A PORTION OF A THESIS PRESENTED TO THE PHILOSOPHICAL
FACULTY OF YALE UNIVERSITY IN CANDIDACY FOR
THE DEGREE OF DOCTOR OF PHILOSOPHY

GORDIAN PRESS, INC.
NEW YORK
1967

Originally Published 1903
Reprinted 1967

Z 2012
. A1 B45
1967

Published by Gordian Press, Inc.

Library of Congress Catalog Card Number 67-21717

Printed in U.S.A. by
EDWARDS BROTHERS, INC.
Ann Arbor, Michigan

PREFACE

THE following pages are designed to give a historical and critical account of all that has been done in the way of translating *Beowulf* from the earliest attempts of Sharon Turner in 1805 down to the present time. As a corollary to this, it presents a history of the text of the poem to the time of the publication of Grein's *Bibliothek der angelsächsischen Poesie* in 1859 ; for until the publication of this work every editor of the poem was also its translator.

It is hoped that the essay may prove useful as a contribution to bibliography, and serve as a convenient reference book for those in search of information regarding the value of texts and translations of *Beowulf*.

The method of treating the various books is, in general, the same. I have tried to give in each case an accurate bibliographical description of the volume, a notion of the value of the text used in making it, &c. But the emphasis given to these topics has necessarily varied from time to time. In discussing literal translations, for example, much attention has been paid to the value of the text, while little or nothing is said of the value of the rendering as literature. On the other hand, in the case of a book which is literary in aim, the attention paid to the critical value of the book is comparatively small. At certain periods in the history of the poem, the chief value of a translation is its utility as a part of the critical apparatus for the interpretation of the poem ; at other periods, a translation lays claim to our attention chiefly as imparting the literary features of the original.

In speaking of the translations which we may call literary, I have naturally paid most attention to the English versions, and this for several reasons. In the first place, *Beowulf* is an *English* poem ; secondly, the number, variety, and importance of the English translations warrant this emphasis ; thirdly, the present writer is unable to discuss in detail the literary and metrical value of translations in foreign tongues. The account given of German, Dutch, Danish, Swedish, French, and Italian versions is, therefore, of a more strictly bibliographical nature ; but, whenever possible, some notion has been given of the general critical opinion with regard to them.

An asterisk is placed before the titles of books which the present writer has not seen.

My thanks are due to the officials of the Library of Yale University, who secured for me many of the volumes here described; to Professor Ewald Flügel of Leland Stanford Junior University, who kindly lent me certain transcripts made for him at the British Museum; and to Mr. Edward Thorstenberg, Instructor in Swedish at Yale University, for help in reading the Danish and Swedish translations.

July, 1902.

TABLE OF CONTENTS

APPENDIX I

INCOMPLETE TRANSLATIONS, AND PARAPHRASES

APPENDIX II

A BIBLIOGRAPHY OF WORKS WHICH TRANSLATE SELECTIONS FROM 'BEOWULF' INTO ENGLISH

APPENDIX III

TWO WORKS NAMED 'BEOWULF'

THE

TRANSLATIONS OF BEOWULF

PRELIMINARY REMARKS ON THE BEOWULF MANUSCRIPT

THE unique manuscript of the *Beowulf* is preserved in the Cottonian Library of the British Museum. It is contained in the folio designated Cotton Vitellius A. xv, where it occurs ninth in order, filling the folios numbered 129 a to 198 b, inclusive.

The first recorded notice of the MS. is to be found in Wanley's Catalog of Anglo-Saxon Manuscripts (Oxford, 1705), Volume III of Hickes's *Thesaurus*. The poem is thus described :—

'Tractatus nobilissimus Poeticè scriptus. Præfationis hoc est initium.'

The first nineteen lines follow, transcribed with a few errors.

'Initium autem primi Capitis sic se habet.'

Lines 53–73, transcribed with a few errors.

'In hoc libro, qui Poeseos Anglo-Saxonicæ egregium est exemplum, descripta videntur bella quæ Beowulfus quidam Danus, ex Regio Scyldingorum stirpe Ortus, gessit contra Sueciæ Regulos.' Page 218, col. b, and 219, col. a.

No further notice was taken of the MS. until 1786, when Thorkelin[1] made two transcripts of it.

In 1731 there occurred a disastrous fire which destroyed a number of the Cottonian MSS. The Beowulf MS. suffered at this time, its edges being scorched and its pages shriveled. As a result, the edges have chipped

[1] See infra, p. 16.

away, and some of the readings have been lost. It does not appear, however, that these losses are of so great importance as the remarks of some prominent Old English scholars might lead us to suspect. Their remarks give the impression that the injury which the MS. received in the fire accounts for practically all of the illegible lines. That this is not so may be seen by comparing the Wanley transcript with the Zupitza *Autotypes*. Writing in 1705, before the Cotton fire, Wanley found two illegible words at line 15—illegible because of fading and rubbing. Of exactly the same nature appear to be the injuries at lines 2220 ff., the celebrated passage which is nearly, if not quite, unintelligible. It would therefore be a safe assumption that such injuries as these happened to the MS. before it became a part of the volume, Vitellius A. xv. The injuries due to scorching and burning are seldom of the first importance.

This point is worth noting. Each succeeding scholar who transcribed the MS., eager to recommend his work, dwelt upon the rapid deterioration of the parchment, and the reliability of his own readings as exact reproductions of what he himself had seen in the MS. before it reached its present ruinous state. The result of this was that the emendations of the editor were sometimes accepted by scholars and translators as the authoritative readings of the MS., when in reality they were nothing but gratuitous additions. This is especially true of Thorpe[1], and the false readings which he introduced were never got rid of until the Zupitza *Autotypes* brought to light the sins of the various editors of the poem. These statements regarding text and MS. will be developed in the following sections of the paper[2].

---

[1] See infra, p. 49.
[2] See infra on Thorkelin, p. 19; Conybeare, p. 29; Kemble, p. 34; Thorpe, p. 51; Arnold, p. 72.

SHARON TURNER'S EXTRACTS

THE History of the Manners, Landed Property, Government, Laws, Poetry, Literature, Religion, and Language of the Anglo-Saxons. By Sharon Turner, F.A.S. London: Longman, Hurst, Rees, & Orme, 1805.

Being Volume IV of the History of the Anglo-Saxons from their earliest appearance above the Elbe, etc. London, 1799–1805. 8°, pp. 398–408.

Second Edition, corrected and enlarged. London: Longman, Hurst, Rees, & Orme, 1807. 2 vols., 4°. *Beowulf* described, Vol. II, pp. 294–303.

Third Edition. London, 1820.

Fourth Edition. London, 1823.

Fifth Edition. (1827 ?)

Sixth Edition. London, 1836.

Seventh Edition. London, 1852.

Reprints: Paris, 1840; Philadelphia, 1841.

Translation of Extracts from the first two Parts.

Points of Difference between the Various Editions.

A part of this may be stated in the words of the author :—

'The poem had remained untouched and unnoticed both here and abroad until I observed its curious contents, and in 1805 announced it to the public. I could then give it only a hasty perusal, and from the MS. having a leaf interposed near its commencement, which belonged to a subsequent part, and from the peculiar obscurity which sometimes attends the Saxon poetry, I did not at that time sufficiently comprehend it, and had not leisure to apply a closer attention. But in the year 1818 I took it up again, as I was preparing my third edition, and then made that more correct analysis which was inserted in that and the subsequent editions, and which is also exhibited in the present.'—Sixth edition, p. 293, footnote.

The statement that the poem had remained untouched and unnoticed is not strictly true. The public had not yet received any detailed information regarding it; but Wanley[1] had mentioned the *Beowulf* in his catalog, and Thorkelin had already made two transcripts of the poem, and was at work upon an edition. Turner, however, deserves full credit for first calling the attention of the English people to the importance of the poem.

In the third edition, of which the author speaks, many improvements were introduced into the digest of the story and some improvements into the text of the translations. Many of these were gleaned from the *editio princeps* of Thorkelin[2]. The story is now told with a fair degree of accuracy, although many serious errors remain: e. g. the author did not distinguish the correct interpretation of the swimming-match, an extract of which is given below. The translations are about as faulty as ever, as may be seen by comparing the two extracts. In the first edition only the first part of the poem is treated; in the third, selections from the second part are added.

No further changes were made in later editions of the History.

Detailed information regarding differences between the first three editions may be found below.

Turner, and his Knowledge of Old English.

Sharon Turner (1768–1847) was from early youth devoted to the study of Anglo-Saxon history, literature, and antiquities. His knowledge was largely derived from the examination of original documents in the British Museum[3]. But the very wealth of the new material which he found for the study of the literature kept him from making a thorough study of it. It is to be remem-

---

[1] See supra, p. 7.   [2] See infra, p. 15.
[3] See the Life of Turner by Thomas Seccombe, *Dict. Nat. Biog.*

bered that at this time but little was known of the peculiar nature of the Old English poetry. Turner gives fair discussions of the works of Bede and Ælfric, but he knows practically nothing of the poetry. With the so-called *Paraphrase* of Cædmon he is, of course, familiar; but his knowledge of *Beowulf* and *Judith* is derived from the unique, and at that time (1805) unpublished, MS., Cotton Vitellius A. xv. Of the contents of the Exeter Book he knew nothing. The Vercelli Book had not yet been discovered. The materials at hand for his study were a faulty edition of Cædmon and an insufficient dictionary. The author, whose interest was of course primarily in history, was not familiar with the linguistic work of the day. It is, therefore, not surprising that his work was not of the best quality.

Lines in the Poem Translated by Turner.

First edition: 18–40; 47–83 a; 199 b–279; 320–324; 333–336; 499–517 a. In the second edition are added: 1–17; 41–46; 83 b–114; 189–199 a; 387–497; 522–528. In the third edition are added: 529–531; 535–558; 607–646; 671–674; 720–738; 991–996; 1013–1042; 1060 b–1068 a; 1159 b–1165 a; 1168 b–1180 a; 1215 b–1226 a; 1240 b–1246 a; and a few other detached lines.

Turner's Account of Beowulf in the First Edition of his History.

' The most interesting remains of the Anglo-Saxon poetry which time has suffered to reach us, are contained in the Anglo-Saxon poem in the Cotton Library, Vitellius A. 15. Wanley mentions it as a poem in which " seem to be described the wars which one Beowulf, a Dane of the royal race of the Scyldingi, waged against the reguli of Sweden [1]." But this account of the contents of the MS. is incorrect. It is a composition more curious and important. It is a narration of the attempt

---

[1] Wanley, Catal. Saxon MS., p. 218.

of Beowulf to wreck the fæthe or deadly feud on Hrothgar, for a homicide which he had committed. It may be called an Anglo-Saxon epic poem. It abounds with speeches which Beowulf and Hrothgar and their partisans make to each other, with much occasional description and sentiment.'—Book vi, chap. iv, pp. 398 ff.

The Story of the Poem as Interpreted by Turner.

[Dots indicate the position of the quotations.]

'It begins with a proemium, which introduces its hero Beowulf to our notice. . . . The poet then states the embarkation of Beowulf and his partisans. . . .' Turner interprets the prolog as the description of the embarkation of Beowulf on a piratical expedition. The accession of Hrothgar to the throne of the Danes is then described, and the account of his 'homicide' is given. This remarkable mistake was caused by the transposition of a sheet from a later part of the poem—the fight with Grendel—to the first section of the poem. The sailing of Beowulf and the arrival in the Danish land are then given. Turner continues: 'The sixth section exhibits Hrothgar's conversation with his nobles, and Beowulf's introduction and address to him. The seventh section opens with Hrothgar's answer to him, who endeavours to explain the circumstance of the provocation. In the eighth section a new speaker appears, who is introduced, as almost all the personages in the poem are mentioned, with some account of his parentage and character.' Then follows the extract given below:

> HUNFERTH spoke
> The son of Ecglafe;
> Who had sat at the foot
> Of the lord of the Scyldingi
> Among the band of the battle mystery.
> To go in the path of Beowulf
> Was to him a great pride;
> He was zealous
> That to him it should be granted
> That no other man

Was esteemed greater in the world
Under the heavens than himself.
'Art thou Beowulf
He that with such profit
Dwells in the expansive sea,
Amid the contests of the ocean?
There yet[2] for riches go!
You try for deceitful glory
In deep waters[3].—
Nor can any man,
Whether dear or odious,
Restrain you from the sorrowful path—
There yet[2] with eye-streams
To the miserable you[4] flourish:
You meet in the sea-street;
You oppress with your hands;
[5]You glide over the ocean's waves;
The fury of winter rages,
Yet on the watery domain
Seven nights have ye toiled.'

After this extract, Turner continues:—'It would occupy too much room in the present volume to give a further account of this interesting poem, which well deserves to be submitted to the public, with a translation and with ample notes. There are forty-two sections of it in the Cotton MS., and it ends there imperfectly. It is perhaps the oldest poem of an epic form in the vernacular language of Europe which now exists.'

[1] Second edition—
  Ever acquired under heaven
  more of the world's glory
  than himself.
[2] Second edition—ye.
[3] Second edition adds—
  Ye sleep not with your ancestors.
[4] Second edition omits.
[5] Second edition reads—
  You glide over the ocean
  on the waves of the sea.

In the second edition the following lines were added :—
' After Hunferthe, another character is introduced :

> Dear to his people,
> of the land of the Brondingi ;
> the Lord of fair cities,
> where he had people,
> barks, and bracelets,
> Ealwith, the son of Beandane,
> the faithful companion
> menaced.
> "Then I think
> worse things will be to thee,
> thou noble one !
> Every where the rush
> of grim battle will be made.
> If thou darest the grendles,
> the time of a long night
> will be near to thee." '

Third Edition.

' Hunferth, "the son of Ecglaf, who sat at the feet of the lord of the Scyldingi." He is described as jealous of Beowulf's reputation, and as refusing to any man more celebrity than himself. He is represented as taunting Beowulf on his exploits as a sea-king or vikingr.

> "Art thou Beowulf,
> he that with such profit
> labours on the wide sea,
> amid the contests of the ocean ?
> There you for riches,
> and for deceitful glory,
> explore its bays
> in the deep waters,
> till you sleep with your elders.
> Nor can any man restrain you,
> whether dear or odious to you,
> from this sorrowful path.
> There you rush on the wave ;
> there on the water streams :

from the miserable you flourish.
You place yourselves in the sea-street;
you oppress with your hands;
you glide over the ocean
through the waves of its seas.
The fury of the winter rages,
yet on the watery domain
seven nights have ye toiled." '

Criticism of the Extracts.

Detailed criticism of the extracts is unnecessary. They are, of course, utterly useless to-day. Sufficient general criticism of the work is found in the preceding sections devoted to a discussion of the author and his knowledge of Old English and of the *Beowulf*.

In the third edition the author presents some criticisms of Thorkelin's text; but his own work is quite as faulty as the Icelander's, and his 'corrections' are often misleading.

Turner is to be censured for allowing an account of *Beowulf* so full of inaccuracy to be reprinted year after year with no attempt at its improvement or even a warning to the public that it had been superseded by later and more scholarly studies.

THORKELIN'S EDITION

DE | Danorum | Rebus Gestis Secul III & IV | Poema Danicum Dialecto Anglosaxonica. | Ex Bibliotheca Cottoniana Musaei Britannici | edidit versione lat. et indicibus auxit | Grim. Johnson Thorkelin. Dr J V. | Havniæ

Typis Th. E. Rangel. | MDCCCXV.   4to, pp. xx, 299, appendix 5.

First Edition.   First Translation (Latin).

Circumstances of Publication.

The words of Wanley cited above[1] did not pass unnoticed in Denmark.   Thorkelin tells us in his introduction that it had long been the desire of Suhm[2], Langebeck, Magnusen, and other Danish scholars to inspect the MS. in the British Museum.   The following is Thorkelin's account of his editorial labors :—

'Via tandem mihi data fuit ad desideratum nimis diu divini vatis Danici incomparabile opus.   Arcta etenim, quæ nos et Britannos intercessit amicitia, me allexit, ut, clementissime annuentibus Augustissimis patriæ patribus CHRISTIANO VII. et FREDERICO VI. iter in Britanniam anno seculi præteriti LXXXVI. ad thesauros bibliothecarum Albionensium perscrutandos facerem. . . . A curatoribus, Musæi Britannici, aliarumque Bibliothecarum, potestas mihi data [est] inspiciendi, tractandi, et exscribendi omnia, quæ rebus Danicis lucem affere possent manuscripta.   Ad quam rem conficiendam viri nostro præconio majores Josephus Planta et Richardus Southgate dicti Musæi Brit. præfecti in me sua officia humanissime contulerunt.   Optimo igitur successu et uberrimo cum fructu domum reversus sum . . .' (pp. viii, ix).

Thorkelin thus obtained two copies of the poem, one made with his own hand, the other by a scribe ignorant of Old English.   These transcripts (still preserved in Copenhagen) formed the basis for Thorkelin's edition. The account of his studies continues :—

'Quæcunque igitur possent hoc meum negotium adjuvare, comparare coepi, magnamque librorum copiam unde quaque congessi, quorum opera carmen aggrederer.   In hoc me sedulum ita gessi, ut opus totum anno MDCCCVII confecerim, idem brevi editurus . . .' (p. xv).

Just at this time, unfortunately, Copenhagen was stormed by the English fleet, and Thorkelin's text and notes were

---

[1] Supra, p. 7.

[2] See also Grundtvig s edition of the text of *Beowulf*, p. xvi.

burned with his library. But the transcripts were saved. Thorkelin renewed his labors under the patronage of Bülow, and at length published in 1815.

Thorkelin, and his Interpretation of the Beowulf.

Grimus Johnssen Thorkelin (or Thorkelsson), 1752–1829, is remembered as a scholar in early Germanic history. He had little beside this knowledge and his general acquaintance with Old Germanic languages to recommend him as an editor of the *Beowulf*. Grundtvig said that the transcript of the *Beowulf* must have been the work of one wholly ignorant of Old English[1]. Thorkelin knew nothing of the peculiar style of Old English poetry; he could recognize neither kenning, metaphor, nor compound. He was not even fitted to undertake the transcription of the text, as the following section will make evident.

We have seen how Sharon Turner[2] could describe the *Beowulf*. Thorkelin seems to have been little better fitted to understand the poem, to say nothing of editing it. He failed to interpret some of the simplest events of the story. He did not identify Scyld, nor understand that his body was given up to the sea, but thought that King Beowulf 'expeditionem suscipit navalem.' He failed to identify Breca, and thought that Hunferth was describing some piratical voyage of Beowulf's. He makes Beowulf reply that 'piratas ubique persequitur et fudit,' and 'Finlandiæ arma infert[3].' He regarded Beowulf as the hero of the Sigemund episode. He quite misapprehended the Finn episode, 'Fin, rex Frisionum, contra Danis pugnat ; vincitur; fœdus cum Hrodgaro pangit ; fidem frangit ; pugnans cadit[4].' He regards Beowulf and a son of Hunferth as participating

---

[1] See *Beowulfs Beorh*, p. xviii.
[2] See supra, p. 11.
[3] See Thorkelin, p. 257.
[4] Ibid., p. 259.

B

in that expedition.   He failed to identify Hnæf, or Hengest,
or Hrothulf, &c.

EXTRACT ¹.

Hunferþ maleode	*Hunferd* loquebatur
Ecglafes bearn	*Ecglavi* filius,
Þe æt fotum sæt	Qui ad pedes sedit
Frean Scyldinga	Domini Scyldingorum,
On band beadu	Emeritus stipendiis
Rune wæs him	Momordit eum
Beowulfes siþ modges	*Beowulfi* itinere elati
Mere faran	Maria sulcando
Micel æfþunca	Magna indignatio,
For þon þe he ne uþe 10	Propterea quod ille nesciret
Þæt ænig oþer man	Ullum alium virum
Æfre mærþa	Magis celebrem
Þon ma middangardes	In mundo
Gehedde under heofenum	Nominari sub coelo
Þon he sylfa eart	Quam se ipsum.
Þu se Beowulf	Tu sis *Beowulfus*,
Se þe wiþ breccan	Qui ob prædas
Wunne on sidne sæ	Geris per latum æquor
Ymb sund flite	Et maria pugnas.
Þær git for wlence 20	Ibi vos ob divitias
Wada cunnedon	Vada explorastis,
And for dol gilpe	Et ob falsam gloriam
On deop wæter	Profundas æquas.
Aldrum neþdon	Annis subacto
Ne mic ænig mon	Non mihi aliquis
Ne leof ne laþ	Amicus aut hostis
Belean mighte.	Objicere potest,
Sorh fullne siþ	Illacrimabiles expeditiones.
Þa git on sund reon.	Ubi vos per æquora ruistis,
Þa git ea gor stream 30	Ibi fluctus sanguinis rivis
Earmum þehton	Miseri texistis.
Mæton mere stræta	Metiti estis maris strata :
Mundum brugdon	Castella terruistis :
Glidon ofer garsecg	Fluitavistis trans æquora.
Geofon yþum	Salis undæ

¹ See Thorkelin, p. 40.

Weol wintris wylm		Fervuerunt nimborum æstu.
Git on wæteris æht		Vos in aquarum vadis
Seofon night swuncon		Septem noctibus afflicti fuistis.
He þe at sunde		Ille cum sundum
Oferflat hæfde	40	Transvolasset,
Mare mægen		Magis intensæ vires
Þa hine on morgen tid		Illum tempore matutino
On heaþo Ræmis		In altam Ræmis
Holm up æt baer		Insulam advexere.
Þonon he gesohte		Deinde petiit
Swæsne.		Dulcem,
Leof his leodum		Charam suo populo
Lond Brondinga		Terram Brondingorum.
Freoþo burh fægere.		Libertate urbem conspicuam
Þær he folc ahte	50	Ibi populo possessam
Burh and beagas		Urbem et opes
Beot eal wiþ		Correpsit. Omne contra
Þe sunu Beanstanes		Tibi filius *Beansteni*
Sode gelæste.		Vere persolvit.

Criticism of the Text.

In order to show how corrupt the text is, I append
a collation of the above passage with the MS.   It may be
added that the lines are among the simplest in the poem,
and call for no emendation.   In passages that present any
real difficulty, Thorkelin is, if possible, even more at fault.

Line   1, *for* maleode *read* maþelode.
   4, *insert period after* Scyldinga.
   9, *insert period after* æsþunca.
   13, *for* middangardes *read* middangeardes.
   15, *for* þon *read* þonne.
   17, *for* breccan *read* brecan (i. e. Brecan).
   25, *for* mic *read* inc.
   27, *for* mighte *read* mihte.
   37, *for* wæteris *read* wæteres.
   38, *for* night *read* niht.
   40, *insert period after* oferflat.

Line 43, *for* heaþo Ræmis *read* heaþoræmes (i.e. Heaþo-
ræmas).

46, *for* Swæsne *read* swæsne ·⚒· (i.e ēđel).

54, *for* sode *read* sođe.

In the composition of his text Thorkelin made all the
errors known to scribes and editors. He misread words
and letters of the MS., although he had two transcripts.
He dropped letters, combinations of letters, and even whole
words. He joined words that had no relation to each
other; he broke words into two or even three parts; he
ignored compounds. He produced many forms the like
of which cannot be found in Old English. One further
example of his great carelessness may be given. The
first line of the poem, which is written in large capitals
in the MS.:—

> Hwæt we Gardena. . . .

Thorkelin perversely transcribed:—

> Hwæt wegar Dena. . . .

and for this combination of syllables he chose the translation:—

> Quomodo Danorum.

There is, of course, no such word as 'wegar' in Old
English.

Of the necessity of punctuation Thorkelin seems to have
been serenely unconscious; he did not even follow the
guides afforded by the MS. Had he done so, he would
have saved himself many humiliating errors. For example,
in the text given above, to have noticed the periods mentioned in the collation would have been to avoid two
glaring instances of 'running-in.'

Criticism of the Translation.

But, in spite of the wretched text, it remained for the
translation to discover the depths of Thorkelin's ignorance.
It will be seen by reading the extract given from the

translation that he did not even perceive that two men were swimming in the sea. It is to be remembered, too, that his error of the 'piratical expedition' is carried on for sixty lines—certainly a triumph of ingenuity. It is useless to attempt a classification of the errors in this version. In the words of Kemble:—

'Nothing but malevolence could cavil at the trivial errors which the very best scholars are daily found to commit, but the case is widely different when those errors are so numerous as totally to destroy the value of a work. I am therefore most reluctantly compelled to state that not five lines of Thorkelin's edition can be found in succession in which some gross fault, either in the transcription or translation, does not betray the editor's utter ignorance of the Anglo-Saxon language.'—Edition of 1835, Introd., p. xxix.

Reception of Thorkelin's Edition.

The book was of value only in that it brought Beowulf to the attention of scholars. The edition was used by Turner, Grundtvig, and Conybeare. I have found the following notices of the book, which will show how it was received by the scholarly world.

TURNER. On collating the Doctor's printed text with the MS. I have commonly found an inaccuracy of copying in every page.—Fifth edition, p. 289, footnote.

KEMBLE, see supra.

THORPE. (The work of the learned Icelander exhibits) 'a text formed according to his ideas of Anglo-Saxon, and accompanied by his Latin translation, both the one and the other standing equally in need of an Œdipus.'—Edition of 1855, Preface, xiv.

See also Grundtvig's criticism in *Beowulfs Beorh*, pp. xvii ff.

GRUNDTVIG'S TRANSLATION

*Bjowulf's Drape. Et Gothisk Helte-digt fra forrige Aar-tusinde af Angel-Saxisk paa Danske Riim ved Nic. Fred. Sev. Grundtvig, Præst. Kjøbenhavn, 1820[1]. 8°, pp. lxxiv, 325.

Bjovulvs-Drapen, et Hoinordisk Heltedigt, fra Anguls-Tungen fordansket af Nik. Fred. Sev. Grundtvig. Anden forbedrede Udgave. Kiøbenhavn. Karl Schønbergs Forlag. 1865. 8°, pp. xvi, 224.

First Danish Translation.   Ballad Measures.

Grundtvig.

Nicolas Frederic Severin Grundtvig (1783–1872) was especially noted as a student of Old Germanic literature. He began his career in 1806 by his studies on the *Edda.* This was followed by a book on Northern Mythology (1810), and by various creative works in verse and prose, the subjects of which were usually drawn from old Danish history. An account of his labors on the *Beowulf* will be found in the following section. His interest in Old English literature continued through his long life, and he was well and favorably known among the scholars of his day.

Circumstances of Publication.

In *Beowulfs Beorh* (Copenhagen, 1861), Grundtvig tells the story of his early translation of the poem. He had always had a passionate interest in Danish antiquities, and was much excited upon the appearance of Thorkelin's text[2]. At that time, however, he knew no Old English,

---

[1] This volume I have never seen. My information regarding it is from a scribe in the British Museum.

[2] See supra, p. 15.

and his friend Rask, the famous scholar in Germanic philology, being absent from Denmark, he resolved to do what he could with the poem himself. He began by committing the entire poem to memory. In this way he detected many of the outlines which had been obscured by Thorkelin. The results of this study he published in the *Copenhagen Sketch-Book* (*Kjøbenhavns Skilderie*), 1815. When Thorkelin saw the studies he was furious, and pronounced the discoveries mere fabrications.

But Rask, upon his return, thought differently, and proposed to Grundtvig that they edit the poem together. They began the work, but when they reached line 925 the edition was interrupted by Rask's journey into Russia and Asia. With the help of Rask's *Anglo-Saxon Grammar* (Stockholm, 1817), Grundtvig proceeded with his translation. By the munificence of Bülow, who had also given assistance to Thorkelin, Grundtvig was relieved of the expense of publication.

Progress of the Interpretation of the Poem.

Grundtvig was the first to understand the story of *Beowulf*. With no other materials than Thorkelin's edition of the text and his own knowledge of Germanic mythology, he discovered the sea-burial of King Scyld, the swimming-match, and the Finn episode. He identified Breca, Hnæf, Hengest, King Hrethel, and other characters whose names Thorkelin had filched from them.

Text Used.

Rask borrowed the original transcripts which Thorkelin had brought from the British Museum, and copied and corrected them. This was the basis of Grundtvig's translation.

Differences between the First and Second Editions.

The principal difference is in the introduction ; but of the nature and extent of changes in the second edition I can give no notion. All my information respecting the first volume is derived from transcripts of certain parts of it sent me from the British Museum. These copies do not reveal any differences between the two translations.

Aim of the Volume, and Nature of the Translation.

We begin by quoting the author's words :—

'I have studied the poem as if I were going to translate it word for word ... but I will not and have not translated it in that way, and I will venture to maintain that my translation is a faithful one, historically faithful, inasmuch as I have never wilfully altered or interpolated anything, and poetically faithful inasmuch as I have tried with all my might vividly to express what I saw in the poem. . . . Whoever understands both languages and possesses a poetical sense will see what I mean, and whoever is deficient in knowledge or sense, or both, may stick to his own view, if he will only let me stick to mine, which may be weak enough, but is not so utterly devoid of style and poetry as little pettifoggers in the intellectual world maintain because they can see very well that my method is not theirs. "I have," said Cicero, "translated Demosthenes, not as a grammarian but as an orator, and therefore have striven not so much to convince as to persuade my readers of the truth of his words " : methinks I need no other defence as regards connoisseurs and just judges, and if I am much mistaken in this opinion, then my work is absolutely indefensible[1].'—Pages xxxiv, xxxv.

In the introduction to his text of 1861, Grundtvig speaks of his theory of translation, saying that he gave, as it were, new clothes, new money, and new language to the poor old Seven Sleepers, so that they could associate freely with moderns. He believed that it was necessary to put the poem into a form that would seem natural and

---

[1] Translation by scribe in British Museum.

attractive to the readers of the day. In so doing he departed from the letter of the law, and rewrote the poem according to his own ideas.

In the second edition the author states that he hopes the poem will prove acceptable as a reading-book for schools. Its value as a text-book in patriotism is also alluded to.

EXTRACT.

SJETTE SANG.

Trætten med Hunferd Drost og Trøsten derover.

Nu *Hunferd* tog til Orde[1],
Og *Egglavs* Søn var han,
Men Klammeri han gjorde
Med Tale sin paa Stand.
Han var en fornem Herre,
Han sad ved Thronens Fod,
Men avindsyg desværre,
Han var ei Bjovulv god;
En Torn var ham i Øiet
Den Ædlings Herrefærd,
Som havde Bølgen pløiet
Og Ære høstet der;
Thi Hunferd taalte ikke,
Med Næsen høit i Sky,
At Nogen vilde stikke
Ham selv i Roes og Ry.

'Er du,' see det var Skosen,
'Den Bjovulv Mudderpram,
Som dykked efter Rosen
Og drev i Land med Skam,
Som kæppedes med *Brække*
Og holdt sig ei for brav,
Dengang I, som to Giække,
Omflød paa vildne Hav!
I vilde med jer Svømmen
Paa Vandet giøre Blæst,
Men drev dog kun med Strømmen,
Alt som I kunde bedst;

[1] Several variations in meter occur in the translation.

For aldrig Det ei keise
Jeg vilde slig en Klik,
Som for den Vendereise
I paa jert Rygte sik.
Paa Landet var I friske,
Men Vand kan slukke Ild,
I svømmed som to Fiske,
Ia, snart som døde Sild;
Da sagtnedes Stoheien,
Der Storm og Bølge strid
Ier viste Vinterveien
Alt i en Uges Tid.
Dog, om end Narre begge,
Kom du dog værst deran,
Thi fra dig svømmed Brække
Og blev din Overmand;
Du artig blev tilbage,
Der han en Morgenstund
Opskvulpedes saa fage
Paa høie Romøs Grund,
Hvorfra sin Kaas han satte
Til *Brondingernas* Land,
Med Borge der og Skatte
Han var en holden Mand;
Der havde han sit Rige,
Og deiligt var hans Slot,
Han elsket var tillige
Af hver sin Undersaat.
Saa *Bjansteens* Søn udførte
Alt hvad han trued med;
Men da du, som vi hørte,
Kom der saa galt afsted,
Saa tør jeg nok formode,
Om end du giør dig kry,
Det giør slet ingen Gode,
Du brænder dig paany;
Ia, vil en Nat du vove
At bie Grændel her,
Da tør derfor jeg love,
Dig times en Ufærd.'

Criticism of the Translation.

The poem departs so far from the text of *Beowulf* that any discussion of its accuracy would be out of place. As has been shown by the section on the nature of the translation, the author had no intention of being true to the letter of the text. Grundtvig's scholarship has been discussed above.

The translation may properly be called nothing more than a paraphrase. Whole sentences are introduced that have no connection with the original text. Throughout the translation is evident the robust, but not always agreeable, personality of the translator. In his preface [1] Grundtvig remarked that he put nothing into his poem that was not historically and poetically true to the original. The statement can only be regarded as an unfortunate exaggeration. Grundtvig's style cannot be called even a faint reflection of the *Beowulf* style. He has popularized the story, and he has cheapened it. There is no warrant in the original for the coarse invective of the extract that has just been cited. In the Old English, Hunferth taunts Beowulf, but he never forgets that his rival is ' doughty in battle' (l. 526). Beowulf is always worthy of his respect. In Grundtvig, the taunting degenerates into a scurrilous tirade. Hunferth calls Beowulf a 'mudscow'; Breca and Beowulf swim like two 'dead herrings.' In like manner the character of Hunferth is cheapened. In *Beowulf* he is a jealous courtier, but he is always heroic. In Grundtvig he is merely a contemptible braggart, 'with his nose high in air,' who will not allow himself to be 'thrown to the rubbish heap.'

The same false manner is retained throughout the poem. In many places it reads well—it is often an excellent

[1] See supra, p. 24.

story. But it can lay no claim to historic or poetic fidelity to the *Beowulf*.

Reception of the Book.

The book fell dead from the press. Grundtvig himself tells us that it was hardly read outside his own house[1]. Thirty years later he learned that the book had never reached the Royal Library at Stockholm. A copy made its way to the British Museum, but it was the one which Grundtvig himself carried thither in 1829. This was doubtless the copy that was read and criticized by Thorpe and Wackerbarth. Both of these scholars spoke of its extreme freedom, but commended its readableness.

CONYBEARE'S EXTRACTS

Illustrations of Anglo-Saxon Poetry. By John Josias Conybeare, M.A., &c. Edited, together with additional notes, introductory notices, &c., by his brother, William Daniel Conybeare, M.A., &c. London : printed for Harding and Lepard, Pall Mall East, 1826. 8°, pp. (viii), xcvi, 287.

Anglo-Saxon Poem concerning the Exploits of Beowulf the Dane, pp. 30–167.

Translation of extracts into English blank verse, with the original text of the extracts, and a literal translation of them into Latin prose.

Circumstances of Publication.

The volume had its origin in the Terminal Lectures which the author gave as Professor of Anglo-Saxon and

---

[1] See *Beowulfs Beorh*, p. xix.

Poetry at Oxford from 1809 to 1812 [1]. We know from an autobiographical note printed in the Introduction [2] that the *Beowulf* was finished in October, 1820. But the book did not appear until two years after the author's death, and the material which it contains is of a slightly earlier date than the title-page would seem to indicate—e.g. the volume really antedates the third edition of Turner's History discussed above [3].

Conybeare, and the Progress of the Interpretation of the Poem.

Conybeare did not edit the entire poem, and apparently never had any intention of so doing. The selections which he translates are based on Thorkelin's text. He revises this text, however, in making his translations, and even incorporates a collation of Thorkelin's text with the MS. (pp. 137–55). This collation, though not complete or accurate, was serviceable, and kept Conybeare from falling into some of the errors that the Icelander had made. He distinguished by an asterisk the MS. readings which were of material importance in giving the sense of a passage, and, in fact, constructed for himself a text that was practically new.

'The text has been throughout carefully collated with the original Manuscript, and the translation of Thorkelin revised with all the diligence of which the editor is capable.'—Page 32.

'Any attempt to restore the metre, and to correct the version throughout, would have exceeded the bounds, and involved much discussion foreign to the purpose of the present work. This must be left to the labours of the Saxon scholar. It is evident, however, that without a more correct text than that of Thorkelin, those labours must be hopeless. The wish of supplying that deficiency, may perhaps

---

[1] See Editor's Prefatory Notice, p. (iii).
[2] See Prefatory Notice, p. (v), footnote.
[3] See supra, pp. 14 f.

apologize for the occupying, by this Collation, so large a space of a work strictly dedicated to other purposes.'—Page 137, footnote.

How much Conybeare improved the text may be seen by comparing his text and Latin translation with those of Thorkelin. The first six lines of the Prolog follow :—

CONYBEARE.	THORKELIN.
Hwæt we Gar-Dena	Hwæt wegar Dena
In ʒear-dagum	In geardagum
Ðeod cyninga	Þeod cyninga
Ðrym ʒefrunon,	Þrym gefrunon
Hu ða Æðelingas	Hu ða æþelingas
Ellen fremodon.—Page 82.	Ellen fremodon.—Page 3.

The translations are even more interesting :—

Aliquid nos *de* Bellicorum Danorum	Quomodo Danorum
In diebus antiquis	In principio
Popularium regum	Populus Regum
Gloriâ accepimus,	Gloriam auxerit,
Quomodo tunc principes	Quomodo principes
Virtute valuerint.	Virtute promoverit.

It will be seen that in these lines Conybeare has at almost every point the advantage over Thorkelin, and is indeed very nearly in accord with modern texts and translations. But the poem yet awaited a complete understanding, for Conybeare could say: ' The Introduction is occupied by the praises of Scefing . . . and of his son and successor Beowulf. The embarkation of the former on a piratical expedition is then detailed at some length. In this expedition (if I rightly understand the text) himself and his companions were taken or lost at sea' (p. 35). And, in general, he misses the same points of the story as Thorkelin, although he craftily refrains from translating the obscurer passages.

Conybeare apparently knew nothing of the critical work of Grundtvig. This is not surprising when we remember that *Kjøbenhavns Skilderie* was probably not known outside of Denmark [1]. Moreover, it is to be remembered that Conybeare's extracts from the *Beowulf* are not really later than Grundtvig's translation, since they were made in the same year, 1820 [2].

Aim of the Volume, and Nature of the Translations.

From the words quoted above with respect to the collation, it will be seen that Conybeare in no way regarded his book as a contribution to Beowulf scholarship. As professor at Oxford, he attempted a literary presentation of the most beautiful parts of the old poetry. His extracts are, in general, nothing more than free paraphrases. Wishing to popularize the *Beowulf*, he used as a medium of translation a peculiarly stilted kind of blank verse. He dressed the poem out in elegant phrases in order to hide the barrenness of the original. Manifestly he feared the roughness, the remoteness of the poem in its natural state. He feared to offend a nation of readers reveling in the medievalism of Scott and Byron. A literal Latin translation was inserted to appease the scholar.

EXTRACT.

'At a single stroke he (Beowulf) cut through the "*ringed bones*" of her neck, and

> Through the frail mantle of the quivering flesh
> Drove with continuous wound. She to the dust
> Fell headlong,—and, its work of slaughter done,
> The gallant sword dropp'd fast a gory dew.
> Instant, as though heaven's glorious torch had shone,
> Light was upon the gloom,—all radiant light
> From that dark mansion's inmost cave burst forth.
> With hardier grasp the thane of Higelac press'd

---

[1] p. 23. Grundtvig is once mentioned in the notes, but the reference is from the editor, not the author.

[2] p. 29.

His weapon's hilt, and furious in his might
Paced the wide confines of the Grendel's hold¹.'

                              Page 58 ; *Beo.*, 1565-75.

LATIN TRANSLATION.

. . . Ossium annulos fregit ; telum per omnem penetravit moribundam carnem. Illa in pavimentum corruit. Ensis erat cruentus, militare opus perfectum. Effulgebat lumen, lux intus stetit, non aliter quàm cum a cœlo lucidus splendet ætheris lampas. Ille per ædes gradiebatur, incessit juxta muros ensem tenens fortiter a capulo Higelaci minister irâ ac constantiâ (*sc.* Iratus et constans animi).

                              Pages 113, 114.

Criticism of the Translations.

The English version is scarcely more than a paraphrase, as may easily be seen by comparing it with the literal translation into Latin. But even as a paraphrase it is unsatisfactory. By way of general criticism it may be said that, while it attains a kind of dignity, it is not the dignity of *Beowulf*, for it is self-conscious. Like *Beowulf* it is elaborate, but it is the elaboration of art rather than of feeling. Moreover, it is freighted with Miltonic phrase, and constantly suggests the Miltonic movement. The trick of verse in line 3 is quite too exquisite for *Beowulf*. The whole piece has a straining after pomp and majesty that is utterly foreign to the simple, often baldly simple, ideas and phrases of the original. Nearly every adjective is supplied by the translator : in Old English the ' sword ' is ' bloody,' in Conybeare the ' gallant sword drops fast a gory dew ' ; the cave becomes a mansion ; the ' floor ' is ' dust '—dust in an ocean cave !—' heaven's candle ' becomes ' heaven's glorious torch.' The poem is tricked out almost beyond recognition. Beowulf assumes the ' grand manner,' and paces ' the Grendel's hold ' like one of the strutting emperors of Dryden's elaborate drama.

¹ Conybeare did not translate the episode of the swimming-match.

KEMBLE'S EDITIONS

The Anglo-Saxon poems of Beowulf, the Traveller's Song, and the Battle at Finnes-burh. Edited together with a glossary of the more difficult words, and an historical preface, by John M. Kemble, Esq., M.A. London: William Pickering, 1833. 8°, pp. xxii, 260. Edition limited to 100 copies.

The Anglo-Saxon Poems of Beowulf, the Traveller's Song, and the Battle of Finnes-burh. Edited by John M. Kemble, Esq., M.A., of Trinity College, Cambridge. Second edition. London: William Pickering, 1835. 8°, pp. xxxii, 263.

A Translation of the Anglo-Saxon Poem of Beowulf, with a copious glossary, preface, and philological notes, by John M. Kemble, Esq., M.A., of Trinity College, Cambridge. London: William Pickering, 1837. 8°, pp. lv, 127, appendix, 179.

First English Translation. Prose.

The 1833 Volume.

A sufficient account of this volume is given by Professor Earle, who says of it :—

'The text was an improvement on Thorkelin, but still very faulty ;—to say nothing of inaccuracies from want of proper oversight as the sheets were passing through the press. The Glossary, though short, was a valuable acquisition ... Of this edition only 100 copies were printed ;—and it was a happy limitation, as it left room for a new edition as early as 1835, in which the text was edited with far greater care. All the rest remained as before, and the Preface was reprinted word for word.'—*Deeds of Beowulf*, pp. xix, xx.

The Text of 1835. Kemble's Scholarship.

But whatever may be said of the text of 1833, there is nothing but praise for the edition of 1835. In this book

C

the poem first had the advantage of a modern scholarly treatment, and for the first time the text of the MS. was correctly transcribed. It received its first punctuation. For the first time it was properly divided into half-lines, with attention to alliteration. The text was freely emended, but the suggested readings were placed in the footnotes, in order not to impair the value of the text as a reproduction of the MS. The necessity for this was made evident by Kemble himself :—

' But while he makes the necessary corrections, no man is justified in withholding the original readings: for although the laws of a language, ascertained by wide and careful examination of all the cognate tongues, of the hidden springs and ground-principles upon which they rest in common, are like the laws of the Medes and Persians and alter not, yet the very errors of the old writer are valuable, and serve sometimes as guides and clues to the inner being and spiritual tendencies of the language itself. The reader will moreover be spared that, to some people, heart-burning necessity of taking his editor's qualifications too much for granted, if side by side he is allowed to judge of the traditional error, and the proposed correction. I have endeavoured to accomplish this end by printing the text, letter for letter, as I found it.'—Preface, pp. xxiv ff.

With this wholesome respect for the tradition of the MS., it is not strange that Kemble's carefully chosen emendations should stand to-day as of high critical value, and that many of them are retained in modern editions of the text [1]. When we compare Kemble's book with Thorkelin's, the advance is seen to be little less than astonishing. Thorkelin's emendations were worse than useless.

Kemble had a full acquaintance with the new science of comparative philology which was developing in Germany under Jakob Grimm. He had corresponded, and later studied, with Grimm, and, according to William Hunt, was the ' recognised exponent ' of his investigations [2]. It is to

[1] See Wyatt's text, lines 51, 158, 250, 255, 599, &c.
[2] See article in the *Dictionary of National Biography*.

Grimm that Kemble dedicates his volumes, and to him that he repeatedly acknowledges his indebtedness. Thus Kemble brought to the study of the poem not only a knowledge of the Old English poetry and prose, but acquaintance with Old Norse, Gothic, Old High German, and Old Saxon. It may sufficiently illustrate his scholarly method to instance examples of his treatment of the unique words in *Beowulf*. Take, e.g., the word *hose* in line 924. This word does not appear elsewhere in Old English; it does not appear in Lye's *Dictionary*, the only dictionary that was at Kemble's disposal. Upon this word Kemble brought to bear his knowledge of the Germanic tongues, and by citing Goth. *hansa*, OHG. *hansa*, &c., derived the meaning *turma*—a process in which he is supported by a modern authority like Kluge. The study of compounds also first began with Kemble. He collected and compared the compounds in *heaðo*. Thus he laid the foundation of all modern studies on the Old English compound.

Further Critical Material Afforded by the Volume of 1837.

In the 1835 volume twenty-three words were illustrated in the above way. But it remained for the 1837 volume to present a complete glossary of the poem, containing also important poetic words not in *Beowulf*. By reason of its completeness and comparative work, it remained the standard commentary on the Old English poetic vocabulary until the appearance of Grein's *Sprachschatz* [1].

Aim of Kemble's Translation.

Like his edition of the text, Kemble's translation is quite independent of any preceding book; like his edition of the text, its aim was faithfulness to the original. He adheres scrupulously to the text, save where the original

[1] See infra, pp. 56 ff.

is unintelligible.   The translation was designed to be used together with the glossary as a part of the apparatus for interpreting the poem.   He therefore made it strictly literal.

‘ The translation is a literal one; I was bound to give, word for word, the original in all its roughness : I might have made it smoother, but I purposely avoided doing so, because had the Saxon poet thought as we think, and expressed his thoughts as we express our thoughts, I might have spared myself the trouble of editing or translating his poem. A few transpositions of words, &c. caused principally by the want of inflections in New English (since we have now little more than their position by which to express the relations of words to one another) are all that I have allowed myself, and where I have inserted words I have generally printed them in italics.’—

Postscript to the Preface, p. l.

EXTRACT.
VIII.

Hunferth the son of Eglaf spake, *he* that sat at the feet of the Lord of the Scyldings ; he bound up [1] a quarrelsome speech : to him was the journey of Beowulf, the proud sea-farer, a great disgust ; because he granted not that any other man should ever have beneath the skies, more reputation with the world than he himself : ‘ Art thou the Beowulf that didst contend with Brecca on the wide sea, in a swimming match, where ye for pride explored the fords, and out of vain glory ventured your lives upon the deep water ? nor might any man, friend or foe, blame [2] your sorrowful expedition : there ye rowed upon the sea, there ye two covered the ocean-stream with your arms, measured the sea-streets, whirled them with your hands, glided over the ocean ; with the waves of the deep [3] the fury of winter boiled ; ye two on the realms of water laboured for a week : he overcame thee in swimming, he had more strength : then at the morning tide the deep sea bore him up on Heathoræmes, whence he sought his own paternal land, dear to his people, the land of the Brondings, where he owned

---

[1] *bound up*, onband, now generally translated ‘ unbind.’
[2] *blame*, belēan, rather ‘ dissuade ’ than ‘ blame.’
[3] *with the waves of the deep*, &c., geofon-yþu weol wintrys wylm, so Kemble reads in his text, and for this reading the translation is correct, but he failed to discern the kenning to ‘ geofon ’ in ‘ wintrys wylm.’

a nation, a town, and rings. All his promise to thee, the son of Beanstan truly performed.'

Criticism of the Translation.

Kemble's scholarship enabled him to get a full understanding of the poem, and thus to make the first really adequate translation of *Beowulf*. He was the first to recognize the significance of kenning, metaphor, and compound. Thus his work is to be commended chiefly because of its faithfulness. All preceding studies had been wofully inaccurate[1]. Kemble's editions became at once the authoritative commentary on the text, and held this position until the appearance of Grein's *Bibliothek* (1857). In this latter book, Kemble's text was the principal authority used in correcting the work of Thorpe[2]. In spite of the fact that this is a literal translation, it sometimes attains strength and beauty by reason of its very simplicity.

ETTMÜLLER'S TRANSLATION

Beowulf. Heldengedicht des achten Jahrhunderts. Zum ersten Male aus dem Angelsächsischen in das Neuhochdeutsche stabreimend übersetzt, und mit Einleitung und Anmerkungen versehen von Ludwig Ettmüller. Zürich, bei Meyer und Zeller, 1840. 8°, pp. 191.

First German Translation. Imitative measures.

Ettmüller.

Ernst Moritz Ludwig Ettmüller (1802–77), at the time of the publication of this book, was professor of the German

---

[1] See supra on Turner, p. 9; Thorkelin, p. 15; Grundtvig, p. 22; Conybeare, p. 28.
[2] See infra, p. 49.

language and literature in the Gymnasium at Zürich. He had already appeared as a translator with a work entitled *Lieder der Edda von den Nibelungen.* Later he edited selections from the *Beowulf* in his *Engla and Seaxna Scôpas and Bôceras* (1850). This text incorporated many new readings. Ettmüller was the first to question the unity of the *Beowulf*, and sketched a theory of interpolations which has since been developed by Müllenhoff. The first announcement of these views is found in the introduction to this translation.

Theory of Translation.

Ettmüller gives full expression to his theories and aims :—

'Vor Allem habe ich so wörtlich als möglich übersetzt, da Treue das erste Erforderniss einer guten Übersetzung ist. Dann aber war mein Augenmerk vorzüglich auf Wohlklang und Verständlichkeit gerichtet. Letztere werden bei Übersetzungen dieser Art nur zu oft vernachlässigt, da manche der Ansicht sind, ihre Arbeit sei um so besser, je treuer sie die äussere Form des Originals in allen Einzelheiten wiedergebe. Aber dieweil diese so mühsam an der Schale knacken, entschlüpft ihnen nicht selten der Kern. Mein Bestreben war demnach keineswegs, z. B. jeden Vers ängstlich dem Originale nachzubilden, so dass die genaueste Übereinstimmung zwischen der Silbenzahl und den Hebungen oder gar dem Klange der Verse Statt fände. Das wäre ohnehin, ohne der deutschen Sprache die schreiendste Gewalt anzuthun, unmöglich gewesen. Ich habe vielmehr darnach mit Sorgfalt gestrebt, die Versbildung des angelsächsischen Gedichtes mir in allen ihren Erscheinungen klar zu machen, und dann frei nach dem gewonnen Schema gearbeitet. Daher kann ich versichern, dass man für jeden Vers meiner Übersetzung gewiss ein angelsächsisches Vorbild findet, wenn auch nicht grade jedesmal die Verse einander decken. Dass dabei übrigens der höheren Rhythmik, d. h. dem ästhetisch richtigen Verhältnisse des Ausdruckes zu dem Ausgedrückten oder, mit Klopstock zu reden, des Zeitausdruckes oder Tonverhaltes (der Bewegung) zu dem Gedanken, überall die grösste Sorgfalt zugewendet ward, das braucht, dünkt mich, keiner besondern Versicherung ; dies aber kann erreicht werden auch ohne knechtische Nachbildung des Originals.'—Page 59.

Text, and Indebtedness to Preceding Scholars.

The translation is founded on Kemble's text of 1835[1], to which the introduction and notes are also indebted.

Like Kemble, Ettmüller was a close student of the works of Jakob Grimm, and his interpretation of obscure lines (especially passages relating to Germanic antiquities) is largely due to the study of such works as the *Deutsche Mythologie* (1833), the *Deutsche Rechtsalterthümer* (1828), and the *Deutsche Sagen* (1816–8). Cf. lines 458, 484.

EXTRACT.

Ecglâfes Sohn Hûnferdh da sagte,
der zu Füssen sass dem Fürsten der Skildinge,
entband Beadurunen — ihm war Beowulfes Beginn,
des muthigen Meergängers, mächtig zuwider ;
ungern sah er, dass ein andrer Mann
irgend Machtruhmes mehr in Mittelgart,
auf Erden äufnete denn er selber — :
' Bist du der Beowulf, der mit Breca kämpfte
600 in sausender See, im Sundkampfe ?
Ihr da aus Übermuth Untiefen prüftet
und aus Tollmuth ihr in tiefem Wasser
das Leben wagtet ; liesset keinen,
nicht Freund noch Feind, da fernen euch
von der sorgvollen That, als zur See ihr rudertet.
Dort ihr den Egistrom mit Armen wandtet,
masset die Meerstrasse, mischtet mit Händen,
glittet über's Geerried (Glanderfluthen
warf Winters Wuth !), in Wassers Gebiet
610 sieben Nächt' ihr sorgtet : Er, Sieger der Wogen,
hatte mehr der Macht, denn zur Morgenzeit ihn
bei Headoræmes die Hochfluth antrug.—
Von dannen er suchte die süsse Heimat,
lieb seinen Leuten, das Land der Brondinge,
die feste Friedeburg, da Volk er hatte,
Burg und Bauge ;—All Erbot wider dich
der Sohn Beanstânes sorglichst erfüllte.'

[1] See supra, p. 33.

Criticism of the Translation.

In his translation Ettmüller followed in the steps of Kemble[1], but he was not slavishly dependent upon him. At times he disagrees with the English scholar (cp. e. g., ll. 468, 522, 1331), and offers a translation of the passage omitted by him, 3069–74. In general, the translation is strictly literal, and follows the original almost line for line.

It was probably well for Ettmüller that he made his translation thus literal. In the history of a foreign-language study there is a period when it is best that a translation should be strictly literal, for such a work is bound to be called into service as a part of the critical apparatus for the interpretation of the tongue. If the early translation is not thus literal, it is sure to be superseded later by the more faithful rendering, as Schaldemose's superseded Grundtvig's in Denmark[2]. It is not until criticism and scholarship have done their strictly interpretative work that a translation is safe in attempting to render the spirit rather than the letter of the original. The reason for this is evident: no real appreciation of the spirit is possible until scholarship has provided the means for discovering it.

By the publication of this volume, therefore, Ettmüller did for German scholarship what Kemble had done for English and Schaldemose was to do for Danish scholarship. Yet he might with propriety have made his work more simple. His translation is disfigured by numerous strange word-combinations which he often transcribed literally from the original, e. g. *beadu-runen* in the third line of the extract. It is safe to say that none but a scholar in Old English would be able to understand this word—if, indeed, we may call it a word. The text is full of such forms. The author

---

[1] See supra, p. 33.
[2] See supra, p. 22, and infra, p. 41 ff.

is obliged to append notes explaining his own translation! He apparently forgets that it is his business as translator to render the difficult words as well as the simple ones. In Ettmüller's case it was especially unfortunate, because it gave others an opportunity to come forward later with simpler, and hence more useful, translations.

Reception of the Translation.

The book had no extraordinary success. A reprint was never called for, and was perhaps hardly to be expected, considering the existence of Kemble's volumes. Moreover, the translation was not accompanied by an edition of the text. Grein [1], the next German scholar, took his inspiration from Kemble [2] and Thorpe [3] rather than from Ettmüller.

SCHALDEMOSE'S TRANSLATION

Beo-wulf og Scopes Widsið, to angelsaxiske Digte, med Oversættelse og oplysende Anmærkninger udgivne af Frederik Schaldemose. Kjøbenhavn, 1847.
Anden Udgave, Kjøbenhavn, 1851. 8°, pp. ii, 188.
Second Danish Translation.

Nature of the Volume, and Indebtedness to Previous Scholars.

In this book the Old English text and the Danish translation were printed in parallel columns. The text, which was taken literally from Kemble [4], need not detain us here. No mention is made of the work of Leo [5], Ettmüller [6], or of the 1837 volume of Kemble, although

---

[1] See infra, p. 55. [2] See supra, p. 33. [3] See infra, p. 49.
[4] See supra, p. 33. [5] See infra, p. 121. [6] See supra, p. 37.

the influence of the latter is evident throughout the book, as will be shown below. The notes are drawn largely from the works of preceding scholars, and in these the author makes an occasional acknowledgement of indebtedness.

The translation is literal. Grundtvig's translation [1] had been so paraphrastic as often to obscure the sense, and always the spirit, of the original. Schaldemose had the advantage of presenting the most modern text side by side with the translation. Thus the book became a valuable *apparatus criticus* for the Danish student.

Schaldemose.

The life of Frederik Schaldemose (1782-1853) was by no means the quiet, retired life of the student. He had, it is true, been professor at the school of Nykjøbing from 1816 to 1825, and later devoted himself to literary work; but a large part of his life had been spent in military service, in which he had had many exciting adventures by land and sea. After leaving his professorship he again entered military service. Later, he devoted his time alternately to literary and commercial work.

His interest in *Beowulf* seems to have been, like that of Thorkelin [2], primarily the interest of the Danish antiquary. In 1846 he had published a collection of Heroic Danish Songs, ancient and modern. It was doubtless a desire to add to this collection that led him to undertake an edition of the *Beowulf*.

It was hardly to be expected that a man whose life had been so unsettled could materially advance the interpretation of Old English poetry.

---

[1] See supra, p. 22.   [2] See supra, p. 15.

EXTRACT.

Hunferd sagde,
Sønnen af Ecglaf ;
han sad ved Scyldinge-
Styrerens Fødder ;
Kiv han begyndte,
thi kjær var ham ikke
Beowulfs Reise,
den raske Søfarers,
1000 men til Sorg og Harme,
thi han saae ei gjærne
at en anden Mand
meer Magtroes havde,
under Himmelens Skyer
end selv han aatte :
Er Du den Beowulf,
der med Breca kjæmped'
paa det vide Hav
i Væddesvømning,
1010 da I af Hovmod
Havet udforsked',
og dumdristige
i dybe Vande
vovede Livet ;
ei vilde Nogen,
Ven eller Fjende,
afvende eders
sorgfulde Tog ;
til Søen I da roed,
1020 vendte med Armene
de vilde Bølger,
maalde Havveien,
med Hænderne brød den,
og svam over Havet
mens Søen vælted
vinterlige Vover ;
saa paa Vandenes Ryg
I strede syv Nætter ;
han, Seirer paa Havet,
1030 aatte meer Styrke,

thi aarle om Morgenen
til Headhoræmes
Havet ham førde;
derfra han søgde
sit Fædrenerige,
feiret af Sine,
Brondinge-Landet
det fagre Fristed,
hvor et Folk han havde,
1040 Borge og Ringe.
Saa blev hvad Beanstans
Søn Dig loved'
sikkerlig opfyldt.

Criticism of the Text and Translation.

There are two good things to be said of this volume: it contains a literal translation, and it is a literal translation from Kemble's text. Being so, it could not be without merit. There was need of a literal translation in Denmark. Grundtvig's version certainly did not fulfil the letter of the law, and Thorkelin's had long since been forgotten.

Schaldemose's dependence upon the translation of Kemble is very evident. In general, the Danish translator is stopped by the same passages that defy the English translator, e.g. the passage which Kemble failed to interpret at line 3075 was duly and loyally omitted by Schaldemose.

I can find no evidence for the reiterated [1] statement that Schaldemose is throughout his translation slavishly indebted to Ettmüller. Certain it is that he avoided those peculiar forms of Ettmüller's translation which are nothing more than a transliteration from the Old English.

Reception of the Volume.

It is a tribute to the Danish interest in Beowulf that Schaldemose's volume soon passed into a second edition.

---

[1] See Wülker, *Ang. Anz.* IV, 69; Wackerbarth's ed. (see infra, p. 45).

But it was not of a character to arouse the interest of scholars in other countries. Thorpe, the next editor of the poem, had never seen it.

The translation, being strictly literal, naturally commanded very little attention even in Denmark; while it was utterly without interest for readers and students in other countries.

WACKERBARTH'S TRANSLATION

Beowulf, an epic poem translated from the Anglo-Saxon into English verse, by A. Diedrich Wackerbarth, A.B., Professor of Anglo-Saxon at the College of our Ladye of Oscott. London: William Pickering, 1849. 8°, pp. xlvi, 159.

Second English Translation. Ballad Measures.

Circumstances of Publication.

In the introduction Wackerbarth gives a full account of the history of the book:—

' With respect to the Work now presented to the Public, shortly after the putting forth of Mr. Kemble's Edition of the Anglo-Saxon Text in 1833 I formed the Design of translating it, and early in 1837 I commenced the Work. Mr. Kemble's second Volume had not then appeared, and I proceeded but slowly, on account of the Difficulty of the Work, and the utter Inadequacy of any then existing Dictionary. I still however wrought my Way onward, under the Notion that even if I should not think my Book, when finished, fit for Publication, yet that the MS. would form an amusing Tale for my little Nephews and Nieces, and so I went through about a Quarter of the Poem when Illness put an entire stop to my Progress. Afterwards, though the Appearance of Mr. Kemble's additional Volume, containing the Prose

Version, Glossary, &c. had rendered the remainder of my Task comparatively easy, other Matters required my Attention, and the MS.
lay untouched until 1842, between which Time and the present it has
been from Time to Time added to and at length completed, and the
whole carefully revised, much being cancelled and retranslated.'—
Introduction, p. viii.

Indebtedness to preceding Scholars.

' In my Version I have scrupulously adhered to the text of Mr. Kemble,
adopting in almost every Instance his Emendations. . . . My thanks are
due to Mr. Kemble . . . to the Rev. Dr. Bosworth . . . who have . . .
kindly answered my Inquiries relative to various Matters connected
with the poem.'— Pages viii, xiv.

Style and Diction.

' I have throughout endeavoured to render the Sense and the Words
of my Author as closely as the English Language and the Restraints
of Metre would allow, and for this Purpose I have not shrunken either
from sacrificing Elegance to Faithfulness (for no Translator is at liberty
to misrepresent his Author and make an old Saxon Bard speak the
Language of a modern Petit Maître) or from uniting English Words
to express important Anglo-Saxon compounds. . . . Some may ask why
I have not preserved the Anglo-Saxon alliterative Metre.   My Reason
is that I do not think the Taste of the English People would at present
bear it.   I wish to get my book read, that my Countrymen may become
generally acquainted with the Epic of our Ancestors wherewith they
have been generally unacquainted, and for this purpose it was necessary
to adopt a Metre suited to the Language ; whereas the alliterative Metre,
heavy even in German, a Language much more fitted for it than ours,
would in English be so heavy that few would be found to labour
through a Poem of even half the Length of the Beówulf's lay when
presented in so unattractive a Garb.'—Pages ix, x.

EXTRACT.

Canto VIII.

But haughty Hunferth, Ecg-láf's Son
Who sat at royal Hróth-gár's Feet
To bind up Words of Strife begun
And to address the noble Geat.

The proud Sea-Farer's Enterprize   5
Was a vast Grievance in his Eyes:
For ill could bear that jealous Man
That any other gallant Thane
On earth, beneath the Heavens' Span,
  Worship beyond his own should gain.   10
'Art thou Beó-wulf,' then he cry'd,
'With Brecca on the Ocean wide
  That didst in Swimming erst contend,
Where ye explor'd the Fords for Pride
And risk'd your Lives upon the Tide   15
  All for vain Glory's empty End?
And no Man, whether Foe or Friend,
Your sorry Match can reprehend.
O'er Seas ye rowed, your Arms o'erspread
The Waves, and Sea-paths measuréd.   20
The Spray ye with your Hands did urge,
And glided o'er the Ocean's Surge;
The Waves with Winter's fury boil'd
While on the watery Realm ye toil'd,
  Thus seven Nights were told,   25
Till thee at last he overcame,
The stronger in the noble Game.
Then him at Morn the billowy Streams
In triumph bare to Heatho-ræmes
From whence he sought his Fatherland,   30
And his own Brondings' faithful Band,
Where o'er the Folk he held Command,
  A City, Rings, and Gold.
His Promise well and faithfully
Did Beanstán's Son perform to thee;   35
And ill I ween, though prov'd thy Might
In Onslaught dire and deadly Fight,
Twill go with thee, if thou this Night
  Dar'st wait for Grendel bold.'

Criticism of the Translation.

Wackerbarth's translation is not to be considered as
a rival of Kemble's[1]—the author did not wish it to be

---

[1] See supra, p. 33.

so considered. Kemble addressed the world of scholars; Wackerbarth the world of readers. Wackerbarth rather resembles Conybeare [1] in trying to reproduce the *spirit* of the poem, and make his book appeal to a popular audience. Wackerbarth had the advantage of basing his translation on the accurate and scholarly version of Kemble; yet Conybeare and Wackerbarth were equally unsuccessful in catching the spirit of the original. The reason for their failure is primarily in the media which they chose. It would seem that if there were a measure less suited to the Beowulf style than the Miltonic blank verse used by Conybeare, it would be the ballad measures used by Wackerbarth. The movement of the ballad is easy, rapid, and garrulous. Now, if there are three qualities of which the *Beowulf* is not possessed, they are ease, rapidity, and garrulity. Not only does the poet avoid superfluous words—the ballad never does—but he frequently does not use words enough. His meaning is thus often vague and nebulous, or harsh and knotted. Nor can the poem properly be called rapid. It is often hurried, and more often insufficient in detail, but it never has sustained rapidity. The kenning alone is hostile to rapidity. The poet lingers lovingly over his thought as if loath to leave it; he repeats, amplifies. The description of Grendel's approach to Heorot is given three times within twenty lines.

Now these features which have just been described Wackerbarth's ballad lines are eminently unfitted to transmit. But there is still another reason for shunning them. They are almost continuously suggestive of Scott. Of all men else the translator of *Beowulf* should avoid Scott. Scott's medievalism is hundreds of years and miles away from the medievalism of *Beowulf*. His is the self-conscious, dramatic, gorgeous age of

---

[1] See supra, p. 28.

chivalry, of knight and lady, of pomp and pride. *Beowulf* is simple to bareness.

It is in such strong picturesque passages as the swimming-match that Wackerbarth's style is worst. There is a plethora of adjectives, scarcely one of which is found in the original; but they are of no avail—they are too commonplace to render the strength and raciness of the original words. There is too much ballad padding—'then he cry'd,' 'at last,' 'well and faithfully,' 'onslaught dire, and deadly fight.' Hunferth prattles. The heroic atmosphere is gone.

In passages calling for calmness, solemnity, or elevation of thought—and there are many such—the easy flow of a verse monotonous and trivial effectually destroys the beauty of the lines.

But in spite of its very evident limitations, Wackerbarth's translation was a move in the right direction. His aim, in his own words, was to 'get his book read,' and he was wise in choosing a medium that would be popular, even if it were not satisfactory to the scholar. It was better to have *Beowulf* according to Wackerbarth than no *Beowulf* at all.

THORPE'S EDITION

The Anglo-Saxon Poems of Beowulf, The Scop or Gleeman's Tale, and the Fight at Finnesburg. With a literal translation, notes, and glossary, &c., by Benjamin Thorpe. Oxford: printed by James Wright, Printer to the University. M.DCCC.LV.

* Reprinted, 1875. 12°, pp. xxxiv, 330.

Third English Translation. Short Lines.

Author's Prefatory Remarks.

'Twenty-four years have passed since, while residing in Denmark, I first entertained the design of one day producing an edition of Beowulf; and it was in prosecution of that design that, immediately on my arrival in England in 1830, I carefully collated the text of Thorkelin's edition with the Cottonian manuscript. Fortunately, no doubt, for the work, a series of cares, together with other literary engagements, intervened and arrested my progress. I had, in fact, abandoned every thought of ever resuming the task : it was therefore with no slight pleasure that I hailed the appearance of Mr. Kemble's first edition of the text of Beowulf in 1833. . . .

'Copies of Mr. Kemble's editions having for some time past been of rare occurrence, I resolved on resuming my suspended labour, and, as far as I was able, supplying a want felt by many an Anglo-Saxon student both at home and abroad. . . .

'My first impulse was to print the text of the poem as it appears in the manuscript, with a literal translation in parallel columns, placing all conjectural emendations at the foot of each page ; but, on comparing the text with the version in this juxta-position, so numerous and so enormous and puerile did the blunders of the copyist appear, and, consequently, so great the discrepance between the text and the translation, that I found myself compelled to admit into the text the greater number of the conjectural emendations, consigning to the foot of the page the corresponding readings of the manuscript. In every case which I thought might by others be considered questionable, I have followed the more usual course, of retaining in the text the reading of the manuscript, and placing the proposed correction at foot. . . .

'Very shortly after I had collated it, the manuscript suffered still further detriment.

'In forming this edition I resolved to proceed independently of the version or views of every preceding editor.'—Pages vii, viii, xii, xiii.

Criticism of Thorpe's Text.

Considering the amount of time that had elapsed between this and the edition of Kemble [1], Thorpe can hardly be said to have made a satisfactory advance. In some respects his edition is actually inferior to Kemble's. It is probable,

---

[1] See supra, p. 33.

for example, that the collation of which the author speaks in his introduction was the one which he had made twenty years before, and that, in taking up his work a second time, he did not trouble himself to revise it. At any rate, the MS. did not receive from Thorpe that respectful attention that it had had from Kemble. Thorpe was more clever than the former scholar in deciphering faded lines of the MS., but he was not always careful to indicate those letters which he actually found there, and those he himself supplied from conjecture. Yet these readings were often of sufficient importance to affect an entire passage, and later scholarship has in many cases deciphered readings whose sense is entirely different from Thorpe's. Thus his edition presents striking divergences from later texts, while no explanation of them is offered in the footnotes. Not only does he frequently incorporate his own readings in the text without noting the MS. forms, but he even makes mistakes in the MS. forms which he does note. A collation of Thorpe's text with the MS. has revealed a carelessness which was all the more reprehensible in that it came from a scholar who was thought to be well-nigh infallible. A few examples of this carelessness are given :—

Line 319 (158)[1], *banan* (misreads MS. in footnote).

487 (241), *Ic* (word emended from *Ie* without noting MS. form).

1160 (578), *hwæþere* (emends without noting the MS. form).

1207 (601), *ac him* (omits a word).

4408 (2201), *hilde hlemmum* (MS. misread in a foot-note. Emendation unnecessary).

At line 2218 the MS., badly mutilated at this point, reads,

> ... *slæpende be syre* ... *de þeofes cræfte.*

[1] The numbers in parentheses are those of Wyatt's text.

In Thorpe's edition the line reads (4443),

> *... slæpende be fire, fyrena hyrde þeófes cræfte.*

Not only does he fail to state that he has changed MS. *sy* to *fi*, but he gives no indication that for the words *fyrena hyrde* there is no room in the MS., and that the reading is entirely of his own making.

In order to afford a comparative estimate of the work of Thorpe and Kemble, I append the texts of each as they appear at what is now line 2000 [1].

THORPE.		KEMBLE.
Þæt is undyrne,		Þ is un-dyrne,
dryhten Higelác,		dryhten Hige-lác,
(uncer) gemeting		... ge-meting
monegum fyra,		monegū fira
hwylce (orleg)-hwíl	5	hwylce ... hwíl
uncer Grendles		uncer Grendles
weard on þám wange,		weard on wange,
þær he worna fela		þær he worna fela
Sige-Scyldingum		síge-(Scyl)dingum
sorge gefremede,	10	sorge ge-fremede,
yrmde tó aldre.		yrmd(o) tó aldre;
Ic þæt eall gewræc,		ic Þ eall ge-wræc,
swá ne gylpan þearf		swá (ne) gylpan dearf
Grendles maga		Grendeles maga
(ǽnig) ofer eordan	15	(ǽnig) ofer eordan
uht-hlem þone,		uht-hlem done,
se þe lengest leofad		(se þe) lengest leofad
ládan cynnes.		ládan cynnes,
Fǽr-bifongen, ...		(fǽr)-bí-fongen.

These selections give a good basis for judging the merits and defects of Thorpe's edition. Thorpe is seen to have the advantage in deciphering certain parts of the text, see e. g. lines 9, 11, 17. On the other hand, Kemble is far more conscientious. Thus at line 13 Thorpe reads *ne* as if it were found in the MS. It is not there, and Kemble is right in inclosing the letters in parentheses. The same

---

[1] Line 3995 in Kemble; 4004 in Thorpe.

thing is true of *Fǽr* in line 19, and Grend*l*es in line 14. Thorpe's emendations in lines 3 and 5 are an advance on Kemble, and are still retained in the text. But Thorpe might have followed Kemble's punctuation in 18 and 19 to his advantage.

EXTRACT.

VIII.

Hunferth spake,
Ecglaf's son,
who at *the* feet sat
of *the* Scyldings' lord ;
unbound *a* hostile speech.
To him was *the* voyage of Beowulf,
the bold sea-farer,
a great displeasure ;
1010 because he grudged
that any other man
ever more glories
of mid-earth
held under heaven
than himself :
'Art thou the Beowulf
who with Breca strove
on *the* wide sea,
in *a* swimming strife,
1020 where ye from pride
tempted *the* fords,
and for foolish vaunt
in *the* deep water
ventured *your* lives?
Nor you any man,
nor friend nor foe,
might blame
for your sorrowful voyage,
when on *the* sea ye row'd,
1030 when ye *the* ocean-stream,
with *your* arms deck'd,
measur'd *the* sea-ways,
with *your* hands vibrated *them*,

> glided o'er *the* main ;
> ocean boil'd with waves,
> with winter's fury :
> ye on *the* water's domain,
> *for* seven nights toil'd.
> He thee in swimming overcame,
> 1040   *he* had more strength,
> when him at morning tide,
> on to Heatho-ræmes
> *the* sea bore up ;
> whence he sought
> *his* dear country,
> *the* beloved of his people,
> *the* Brondings' land,
> *his* fair, peaceful burgh,
> where he *a* people own'd,
> 1050   *a* burgh and rings.
> All *his* promise to thee
> Beanstan's son
> truly fulfil'd.

Criticism of the Translation.

This being a strictly literal translation, the reader is referred to the sections on the text for a valuation and criticism. It is a question whether there was need for another literal rendering in England at this time. Kemble's translation was not yet out of date, and with Thorpe's new glossary the student had a sufficient apparatus for the interpretation of the poem.

Some German scholars have discovered that the short lines in which Thorpe's translation is couched are imitative of the Old English measure. I am unable to agree with them. Probably any short-line translation would *ipso facto* assume a choppiness not dissimilar to the Old English, and probably plenty of lines could be discovered which correspond well enough to the 'five types,' but the agreement seems purely fortuitous. It is quite unlikely that Thorpe intended any imitation.

Influence of Thorpe's Edition.

The influence of this edition has been considerable. It was the principal authority used by Grein[1] and Heyne[2] in constructing their texts. Thus its influence was felt in all texts down to the publication of the Zupitza *Autotypes* (1882). Thomas Arnold[3] copied the text almost word for word.

GREIN'S TRANSLATIONS

Dichtungen der Angelsachsen, stabreimend übersetzt von C. W. M. Grein. Erster Band. Göttingen : Georg H. Wigand, 1857. 8°, Beowulf, pp. 222–308. Zweite (Titel-) Auflage, 1863.

Beowulf. Stabreimend übersetzt von Professor Dr. C. W. M. Grein. Zweite Auflage. Kassel: Georg H. Wigand, 1883. 8°, pp. 90.

Second German Translation. Imitative Measures.

Grein's Preparation for Scholarly Work.

Christian Wilhelm Michael Grein[4] (1825–77) was eminently well fitted for the editing and translating of Old English poetry. He possessed a natural aptitude for the study of Germanic Philology, and had the advantage of studying with an excellent professor, Franz Eduard Christoph Dietrich (1810–83), in the University at Marburg. As early as 1854 he began his labors as a translator of Old English poetry with a version of the *Phoenix*, 'Der Vogel Phoenix : ein angelsächsisches Gedicht, stabreimend über-

---

[1] See infra, p. 55.   [2] See infra, p. 63.
[3] See infra, p. 71.
[4] For biographical facts see Grein-Wülker, *Bibliothek*, Band III, 2te Hälfte, p. vii.

setzt,' Rinteln, 1854. In the same year he printed a translation of the *Heliand*.

In 1855 he assumed the position of Praktikant at the
Kassel Landesbibliothek. Here he was able to devote
a large part of his attention to the study of Old English,
acquiring a familiarity with the poetry of that tongue which
it has seldom been the fortune of a scholar to surpass. He
formed the design of editing and translating the entire
body of Old English poetry and appending to it a complete glossary which should not only give the meanings of
the words, but instance every occurrence of the word.
This design he carried out between the years 1857 and
1864.

Grein's Texts.

The text of *Beowulf* is found in Grein's *Bibliothek der
angelsächsichen Poesie*, Erster Band, Göttingen, 1857,
where it occupies pp. 255–341. A second edition, several
times re-edited, is *Beovulf, nebst den Fragmenten Finnsburg und Waldere*, Kassel und Göttingen, 1867.

Grein never saw the MS. of the poem[1]. He based his
text on a collation of all the preceding editions. This was
unfortunate, because, had Grein seen the MS., he would
doubtless have hastened to make a correct transcription
of it. As it was, his edition necessarily shares some of the
faults of its predecessors, since the text had never yet been
accurately transcribed. A simple illustration of this defect
may be seen by examining line 2218 of the text, where
Grein reads,

be fire, fyrena hyrde,

following Thorpe[2]. As has been pointed out, this is an
impossible reading, and one for which there is no justifica-
tion in the MS. Thorpe, however, had presented it as the
MS. reading, and Grein could not but copy it.

---

[1] See Grein-Wülker, *Bibliothek*, Vorrede.
[2] See supra, p. 52.

Like Kemble, Grein had a supreme respect for the readings of the MS., and he announced his intention of following this reading wherever possible :—

'Bei der Behandlung des Textes galt als erste Pflicht, handschriftliche Lesarten, wo es nur immer möglich war, zu retten und namentlich auch manche angezweifelte, den Lexicis fremde Wörter als wolbegründet nachzuweisen : nur da, wo Verderbniss auf der Hand liegt, habe ich mir mit der grössten Vorsicht Aenderungen erlaubt oder bereits von Andern vorgeschlagene Aenderungen aufgenommen, wobei ich mich möglichst eng an das handschriftlich gebotene anzuschliessen suchte.'—Vorwort, iv. (*Bibl.*).

This was wise. Since the days of Kemble, emendation had become unnecessarily frequent. We have seen in what a light-hearted way Thorpe spoke of the 'blunders of the scribes,' and how careless he was in the preparation of his text. The dialect had not yet received proper attention, and the copyists were blamed for errors that they never made.

Grein was extremely clever in filling the lacunae of the MS., and his conjectural emendations are frequently retained by later editors.

Still another improvement which he introduced was the full punctuation of the text ; this was superior to any that had preceded it. In previous editions defective punctuation had obscured the sense of the lines ; here it was made a factor in their interpretation.

Theory of Translation.

Grein's theory of translation is sufficiently expressed in the Vorrede to the *Dichtungen* :—

'Die Sammlung von metrischen Uebersetzungen angelsächsischer Dichtungen, deren erster Band hiermit der Oeffentlichkeit übergeben wird, soll einen doppelten Zweck erfüllen. Einerseits betrachte ich dieselben als eine wesentliche Ergänzung, gleichsam als fortlaufenden Commentar zu meiner gleichzeitig in demselben Verlag erscheinenden Textausgabe der angelsächsischen Dichter, indem sie meine Interpreta-

tion der Originaltexte, worin ich oft von meinen Vorgängern abweiche,
einfach vor Augen legen.   Andrerseits aber bezweckte ich dadurch die
Bekanntschaft mit den in vieler Beziehung so herrlichen dichterischen
Erzeugnissen des uns engverwandten englischen Volkes aus der Zeit
vor dem gewaltsamen Eindringen des romanischen Elements durch
die normannische Eroberung auch in weiteren Kreisen anzubahnen,
was sie sowol nach ihrem Inhalte als auch nach der poetischen
Behandlung des Stoffes gewiss in hohem Grade verdienen.   Daher
war ich eifrigst bemüht, die Uebersetzung dem Original in möglichster
Treue nach Inhalt, Ausdruck und Form eng anzuschliessen: namentlich suchte ich, soweit es immer bei dem heutigen Stande unserer
Sprache thunlich war, auch den Rhythmus des Originals nachzubilden,
wobei es vor allem auf die Beibehaltung der eigentümlichen Stellung
der Stabreime ankam, ein Punkt, der bei der Uebertragung alter
Alliterationspoesien nur zu oft vernachlässigt wird.'—Vorrede, iii.

Differences between the two Editions.

The second edition of the translation (see supra, p. 65)
was edited from Grein's 'Handexemplar' of the *Dichtungen*
after his death by Professor Wülker, who has also re-edited
the text of the *Bibliothek*.   The differences are seldom
more than verbal, and are largely in the early parts of the
poem.   The second edition is, of course, superior.

EXTRACT.
III.

Darauf sprach Hunferd, Ecglafs Sohn,
der zu den Füssen sass dem Fürst der Skildinge,   500
entband Streitrunen, (ihm war Beowulfs Reise
des mutigen Seefahrers sehr zum Aerger,
da er durchaus nicht gönnte, dass ein anderer Mann
je mehr des Ruhmes in dem Mittelkreise
besässe unterm Himmel, denn er selber hatte):   505
'Bist du der Beowulf, der einst mit Breka schwamm
im Wettkampfe durch die weite See,
wo in Verwegenheit ihr die Gewässer prüftet
und aus tollem Prahlen in die tiefen Fluten
wagtet euer Leben?   Nicht wehren konnt' euch beiden   510
weder Lieb noch Leid der Leute einer

die sorgenvolle Fahrt, als in den Sund ihr rudertet,
wo ihr den Oceansstrom mit euren Armen decktet,
die Holmstrassen masset, mit den Händen schluget
und über den Ocean glittet: der Eisgang des Winters   515
wallete in Wogen; in des Wassers Gebiet
plagtet ihr euch sieben Nächte. Im Schwimmspiel überwand er dich:
er hatte mehr der Macht; zur Morgenzeit
trug ihn der Holm da zu den Headorämen.
Von dannen suchte er die süsse Heimat   520
lieb seinen Leuten, das Land der Brondinge,
die liebliche Friedeburg, wo er sein Volk hatte,
Burg und Bauge. Da hatte all sein Erbot wider dich
vollbracht in Wahrheit Beanstans Sohn[1].'

Criticism of the Translation.

The translation is a literal line-for-line version. Its superiority to its predecessors is, therefore, one with the superiority of the text on which it is founded.

The translation became at once the standard commentary on *Beowulf*, and this position it retained for many years. It is still the standard literal translation in Germany, none of the later versions having equaled it in point of accuracy.

SIMROCK'S TRANSLATION

Beowulf. Das älteste deutsche Epos. Uebersetzt und erläutert von Dr. Karl Simrock. Stuttgart und Augsburg: J. G. Cotta'scher Verlag, 1859. 8°, pp. iv, 203.

Third German Translation. Imitative Measures.

Simrock.

Dr. Karl Simrock (1802–1876) brought to the translation of *Beowulf* the thorough knowledge of a scholar,

[1] The second edition presents no variation from this save the omission of the comma in line 501.

the fine feeling and technique of a poet, and an enviable reputation as a translator of Old German poetry. At the time when he made his translation of *Beowulf*, he was Professor of Old German Literature at Bonn, whither he had been called because of his contributions to the study of Old German mythology. His title to remembrance rests, however, on his metrical rendering of the *Nibelungen-lied*, a work which, in 1892, had passed into its fifty-second edition. As an original poet, Simrock is remembered for his *Wieland der Schmied* (1835), and *Gedichte* (1844).

Object of the Translation.

Simrock wished to do for *Beowulf* what he had done for the *Nibelungenlied*, *Walther von der Vogelweide*, and *Der arme Heinrich*. He objected to the too literal work of Ettmüller[1] and Grein[2], hoping in his own work to make the poem readable and to dispense with a 'note for every third word':

'Geist und Stimmung einer fernen Heldenzeit anklingen zu lassen, und doch dem Ausdruck die frische Farbe des Lebens zu verleihen.'— Vorrede, iii.

In this ambition he was justified by his success as a translator of Old German poetry.

Nature of the Translation.

The diction of the version is, on the whole, characterized by simplicity and ease. Yet the author, like many another translator of Old English, tries to give his style an archaic tinge by preserving the compound forms characteristic of that language, such as Lustholz, Aelgelage, Kampfrunen, a fault that Ettmüller had carried to excess. These forms he sometimes used to the exclusion of simpler, or even

[1] See supra, p. 37.   [2] See supra, p. 55.

more literal, words. The nature of the German language, however, keeps these from being as repulsive as they are in English, but they are sufficiently strange to mystify and annoy the reader. The feature of his translation for which Simrock was most concerned was the measure :

'Vor Allem aber den Wohllaut, der echter Poesie unzertrennlich verbunden ist, das schien mir die erste Bedingung, damit der Leser . . . den Sinn ahne und von der Schönheit des Gedichtes ergriffen von Blatt zu Blatt getragen werde. Nur so glaubte ich eine tausendjährige Kluft überbrücken und dieser mit Angeln und Sachsen ausgewanderten Dichtung neues Heimatsrecht bei uns erwerben zu können.'—Vorrede, iii, iv.

He also preserved alliteration, believing that a fondness for that poetic adornment may be easily acquired, and that it is by no means inconsistent with the genius of modern tongues.

Relation of Translation and other Parts of the Book.

The notes to the translation contain discussions of the episodes and of the mythological personages of the poem. There is a discussion of the poetic worth of *Beowulf*, and an argument for the German origin of the poem. But the translation is the *raison d'être* of the volume, and other parts are strictly subordinated to it. The Finnsburg fragment is inserted at the end of section 16. As the author does not wish to disturb the order of *Beowulf*, he is obliged to place the poem at the end of the Finnsburg episode (in *Beowulf*), a very ill-chosen position, where it can only confuse the general reader more than the obscure lines to which it is related. This practice of inserting the Finnsburg fragment, lately revived by Hoffmann [1], has been generally repudiated.

[1] See infra, p. 99.

Text, and Indebtedness to Preceding Scholars.

The text followed is Grein's (1857)[1]. The translator
acknowledges his indebtedness to the versions of Ettmüller
and Grein.

EXTRACT.

8. HUNFERD.

Da begann Hunferd,   Ecglafs Sohn,
Der zu Füssen sass   dem Fürsten der Schildinge,
Kampfrunen zu entbinden :   ihm war Beowulfs Kunft,
Des kühnen Seeseglers,   schrecklich zuwider.
Allzu ungern sah er,   dass ein anderer Mann
In diesem Mittelkreis   mehr des Ruhmes
Unterm Himmel hätte   als Hunferd selbst :

  ' Bist du der Beowulf,   der mit *Breka* schwamm
Im Wettkampf einst   durch die weite See ?
Wo ihr tollkühn   Untiefen prüftet,
Mit vermessnem Muth   in den Meeresschlünden
Das Leben wagtet ?   Vergebens wehrten euch
Die Lieben und Leiden,   die Leute zumal
So sorgvolle Reise,   als ihr zum Sunde rudertet,
Das angstreiche Weltmeer   mit Armen decktet,
Die Meerstrassen masset,   mit den Händen schlugt
Durch die Brandung gleitend ;   aufbrauste die Tiefe
Wider des Winters Wuth.   Im Wasser mühtet ihr
Euch sieben Nächte :   da besiegt' er dich im Schw mmen.
Seiner Macht war mehr :   in des Morgens Frühe
Hob ihn die Hochflut   zu den *Headorämen.*
Von dannen sucht' er   die süsse Heimat,
Das Leutenliebe,   das Land der *Brondinge,*
Die feste Friedensburg,   wo er Volk besass,
Burg und Bauge.   Sein Erbieten hatte dir
Da *Beanstans* Geborner   vollbracht und geleistet.'

Criticism of the Translation.

Simrock's translation is commendable for its faithfulness.
It is, moreover, a simple and readable version, though in

[1] See supra, p. 56.

these respects it is not equal to Heyne's rendering which was to follow it ; but it was easily superior to Grein's. Yet, in spite of this, the book is not well known among German translations, and has never passed into a second edition. This is surprising when we consider the success of Simrock's previous translations. The partial failure is accounted for by two facts : (1) Simrock's reputation as a scholar was not equal to that of Grein or Heyne, nor had he the advantage of editing the text ; (2) the measure which the translation employed has never been popular among readers. No German translation in imitative measures, with the single exception of Grein's (which has made its appeal as a scholarly work and not as a piece of literature), has ever passed into a second edition ; while versions couched in iambic lines or Nibelungen meters have been reprinted.

HEYNE'S TRANSLATION

Beowulf. Angelsächsisches Heldengedicht übersetzt von Moritz Heyne. Paderborn : Druck und Verlag von Ferd. Schöningh, 1863. 12°, pp. viii, 127.

Zweite Auflage. Paderborn : Schöningh, 1898. 8°, pp. viii, 134.

Fourth German Translation. Iambic Pentameter.

Heyne.

The name of Moritz Heyne is one of the most illustrious in the history of Beowulf scholarship. The Heyne editions of the text[1] have been standard for nearly forty years,

---

[1] There have been six—1863, 1868, 1873, 1879, 1888, 1898 ; the last two are by Dr. Adolf Socin.

while the translation has been recently reprinted (1898).
Beside his work on the *Beowulf*, this scholar was to become prominent as editor of the *Heliand* and of *Ulfilas*,
and as one of the staff appointed to complete Grimm's
Dictionary.

At the time when he printed his edition of the *Beowulf*,
Heyne was a student at Halle, and but twenty-six years
of age (born 1837)[1]. In his work he had some assistance
from Professor Leo[2] of Halle.

Relation of Text and Translation.

The translation was founded on the text of 1863. At
the time it was by far the best edition that had yet
appeared. It was furnished with an excellent glossary.
The text had the advantage of the valuable work done by
Grundtvig[3] in collating the two transcripts made by Thorkelin[4]. It thus came a stage nearer the MS. readings
than any other existing edition, while it avoided the unnecessary conjectures of the Danish editor.

Heyne's text having been five times re-edited, the first
edition of the translation often fails to conform to readings
which have been introduced into the text in later editions ;
but the free nature of the translation makes this of no
great importance.

Differences between the First and Second Editions of the Translation.

The differences between the two editions are not of
much importance. The translation is in general, though
not always, brought up to the late editions of the text,

---

[1] Heyne is at present Professor in the University of Göttingen.
[2] See infra, p. 121.
[3] In *Beowulfs Beorh*. See also supra, p. 22.
[4] See supra, p. 16.

and some changes are made for the improvement of the meter. The first edition contains 3201 lines; the second 3207. The theory and aim of the translation are not changed at all.

Aim of Heyne's Translation.

In this translation of the *Beowulf*, Heyne attempts to popularize what he considers the most beautiful of the Old English poems. He says of it—

'Es ist nicht die erste, die ich biete; gleichwol hoffe ich es werde die erste sein, die auch einem grössern Publicum, das noch nicht Gelegenheit hatte, sich mit den ältern Dialecten unserer Sprache zu beschäftigen, verständlich ist. Die ältern deutschen Uebersetzer haben, bei allen Verdiensten ihrer Arbeit, unserer neuhochdeutschen Muttersprache teilweise übel mitgespielt.'—Vorwort, iii.

With this in view, Heyne put his translation out in a form that would make it accessible to all. This was in itself an innovation. The works of Ettmüller[1] and Simrock[2] had been in a more elaborate *format*, while Grein's translation[3] was not only expensive, but encumbered with other work, and intended primarily for the scholar.

Nature of the Translation.

Heyne chose a new medium for his version, the unrimed iambic line. His aim being to get his book read, he avoided a literal translation, and rendered with commendable freedom, though not with inaccuracy. He used no strange compounds, and shunned an unnatural verse. Thus he produced the most readable translation that has ever appeared in Germany. Of his own attempt he says—

'Die vorliegende Uebertragung ist so frei, dass sie das für uns schwer oder gar nicht genau nachzubildende alliterierende Versmass des Originals gegen fünffüssige Iamben aufgibt, und zu Gunsten des

[1] See supra, p. 37.   [2] See supra, p. 59.
[3] See supra, p. 55.

E

Sinnes sich der angelsächsischen Wort- und Satzstellung nicht zu ängstlich anschmiegt; dagegen auch wieder so genau, dass sie hoffentlich ein Scherflein zum vollkommenern Verständniss des Textes beitragen wird.'—Vorwort, iii.

Heyne's theory of translation is one that has been very little in vogue in Germany. He has been criticized on all sides for his freedom. Yet the criticism is undeserved. Heyne is never paraphrastic—he never adds anything foreign to the poem. He merely believes in translating the obscure as well as the simple ideas of his text. His ' freedom ' seldom amounts to more than this—

> Hē bēot ne āleh, l. 80 (he belied not his promise)
> Was er gelobt, erfüllt er.

He occasionally inserts a word for metrical reasons, and sometimes, in the interests of clearness, a demonstrative or personal pronoun, or even a proper name (cf. l. 500 of the extract).

EXTRACT.

IX.

Da sagte Hunferd, Ecglafs Sohn, der Hrodgar	500
zu Füssen sass, dem Herrn der Schildinge,	
des Streites Siegel löste er (denn sehr	
war Beowulfes Ankunft ihm verhasst,	
des kühnen Meerbefahrers; er vergönnte	
es Niemand, mehr des Ruhmes als er selber	505
sich unterm Himmel jemals zu erwerben):	
' Bist du der Beowulf, der einst mit Breca	
sich auf der weiten See im Schwimmkampf mass,	
als ihr euch kühnlich in die Tiefen stürztet,	
und mit verwegnen Brüsten euer Leben	510
im tiefen Wasser wagtet? Niemand konnte,	
nicht Freund, nicht Feind, des mühevollen Weges	
euch hindern. Da schwammt ihr hinaus in See,	
wo ihr die wilde Flut mit Armen decktet,	
des Wassers Strassen masset und die Hände	515
die Wogen werfen liesst; so glittet ihr	
hin übers Meer. Die winterlichen Wellen,	

sie giengen hoch. Der Tage sieben mühtet
ihr euch im Wasser : jener überwand dich
im Schwimmen, denn er hatte grössre Kraft.   520
Da trug die Hochflut ihn zur Morgenzeit
auf zu den Hadorämen, von wo aus er,
der seinem Volke liebe, seinen Erbsitz
im Land der Brandinge, die schöne Burg
erreichte. Dort besass er Land und Leute   525
und Schätze. Was er gegen dich gelobt,
das hatte Beanstans Sohn fürwahr erfüllt.'

The extract illustrates sufficiently the characteristics of
Heyne's rendering. In the first place, attention may be
called to the extreme freedom of the verse, a freedom
which at times makes the composition verge upon prose.
In the second place, the translation of the Old English
phrase *beadu-runen onband* should be noticed, and compared with the translations of Ettmüller, Grein, and Simrock,
who have respectively—

> *entband beadurunen*
> *entband Streitrunen*
> *Kampfrunen . . . entbinden.*

Heyne is the only one who translates the phrase in such
a way as to make the words intelligible to a reader unacquainted with Old English. Finally, it should be noticed
that the translation is quite as accurate as those which
preceded it. Heyne certainly succeeded in his attempt
to make the poem more intelligible to the general reader
than it had ever been before. While not so serviceable to
the scholar as Grein's translation, it is undoubtedly the
most enjoyable of the German versions.

VON WOLZOGEN'S TRANSLATION

Beovulf (Bärwelf). Das älteste deutsche Heldengedicht. Aus dem Angelsächsischen von Hans von Wolzogen. Leipzig: Philipp Reclam, jun. (1872?). Volume 430 of Reclam's Universal-Bibliothèk. Small 8°, pp. 104. Fifth German Translation. Imitative Measures.

Concerning the Translator.

Hans von Wolzogen (born 1848), popularly known as a writer on the Wagnerian operas and as conductor of the *Bayreuther Blätter*, translated three Germanic poems for Reclam's 'Bibliothek': *Beowulf*, 1872, *Der arme Heinrich*, 1873, and the *Edda*, 1877. There is no evidence that he had any *special* interest in Old English studies.

Aim of the Volume.

As expressed in the 'Vorbemerkung,' the aim of the translator was (1) to provide a readable translation 'für unser modernes Publicum,' and (2) to make a convenient handbook for the student, so that the beginner, with Grein's text[1] and the present translation, might read the *Beowulf* with no very great difficulty. So von Wolzogen made his version 'more literal than Heyne's, but freer than Simrock's' (p. 1).

Nature of the Translation.

The translation is in alliterative measures, called by the translator imitative of the Old English. Von Wolzogen is concerned for this feature of his work, and is at pains to

[1] See supra, p. 55.

give what he considers a full account of the original verse as well as a lengthy defence of alliteration. Archaic touches are occasional. The names are 're-translated into German' according to a system of which, apparently, von Wolzogen alone holds the key:—

'... diese angelsächsische Form selbst nur eine Uebertragungsform aus den ursprünglich deutschen Namen ist, wobei manch Einer sogar sinnlos verdreht worden, wie z. B. der Name des Helden selbst, der aus dem deutschen Bärwelf, Jungbär, zum Beovulf, Bienenwolf, gemacht worden war.'—Vorbemerkung, p. 5.

The account of the Fall of Hygelac and of Heardred, 2354-96, is shifted to line 2207 (p. 75).

Text Used.

The translation is apparently founded on one of Grein's texts[1], but the work is so inaccurate that exact information on this point is impossible from merely internal evidence.

EXTRACT.

DRITTER GESANG.

HUNFRID.

So sagte Hunfrid[2], der Sohn des *Eckleif*,
Dem Schildingenfürsten zu Füssen gesessen,
Kampfrunen entbindend (es kränkte des *Bärwelf*
Muthige Meerfahrt mächtig den Stolzen,
Der an Ehren nicht mehr einem andern Manne   5
Zu gönnen gemeint war im Garten der Mitte,
Als wie unter'm Himmel erworben er selbst!) :
'Bist du der *Bärwelf*, der mit *Brecht* bekämpfte
Auf weiter See im Wetteschwimmen,
Da übermüthig und ehrbegierig   10
Eu'r Leben ihr wagtet in Wassertiefen,

[1] See Vorbemerkung, p. 3.
[2] The italics, save those used for proper names (which are von Wolzogen's), indicate inaccurate renderings.

Die beid' ihr durchschwammt? Da brachte zum Schwanken
Den Vorsatz der furchtbaren Fahrt euch Keiner
Mit Bitten und Warnen, und Beide durchtheiltet
Mit gebreiteten Armen die Brandung ihr rudernd,   15
Durchmasset das Meer mit *meisternden* Händen
Auf wogenden Wegen, während der Wirbelsturm
Rast' in den Well'n, und *ihr rangt mit* dem Wasser
Durch sieben Nächte. Der Sieger im Neidspiel
Zeigte sich mächt'ger; zur Zeit des Morgens   20
Riss zu den Haduraumen die Flut ihn ;
ins eigene Erbe enteilt' er von dort,
Zum Lande der Brandinge, lieb seinen *Mannen,*
Zur bergenden Burg. Da gebot er dem Volke
Schlossreich und schatzreich. Wie geschworen, so hielt   25
Sein Versprechen dir redlich der Sprössling des *Bonstein.*'

Criticism of the Translation.

Von Wolzogen's translation is hardly trustworthy. A
specimen of his free interpretation of the *Beowulf* diction
may be seen in the footnote on page 13, where he defines
horngēap (i. e. 'with wide intervals between its pinnacles of
horn ') as 'hornreich,' and translates *hornreced*, 'Hornburg.'
Inaccurate renderings of the Old English have been noted
above in italics. They reveal an especial difficulty with the
kenning, a device which von Wolzogen apparently did not
understand, since the entire translation shows an attempt
to interpret the kenning hypotactically. Had the translator
been making a paraphrase, inaccuracies like 'muthige
Meerfahrt' and 'ihr rangt mit dem Wasser' might be
excused ; but in a translation which was avowedly literal
(more literal than Heyne's) they appear to be due to
nothing less than ignorance and carelessness. To give
one example from the thousand that bear out the truth of
this statement, we may cite line 561 (p. 27),

Ic him þēnode
deoran sweorde   swā hit gedēfe wæs.

which is translated,

> dawider doch diente
> Mein treffliches Schwert, das treu mir beistand. (p. 27.)

This is not paraphrase; it is sheer misapprehension of the Old English.

A similar misapprehension is seen in line 15 of the extract,

> Mit Bitten und Warnen,

which we are asked to accept as a translation for

> ne lēof nē lāđ. (l. 511.)

The verse of von Wolzogen's translation is the poorest of the German attempts at imitative measures. The translator is obliged at times to append footnotes explaining the scansion of his lines (see pp. 33, 34, 65, 91). The cesura is frequently not in evidence (cf. lines 14 and 22, both of which are also metrically incorrect); the lines are often deficient in length (p. 29, line 26; p. 31, line 19; p. 32, line 19).

ARNOLD'S EDITION

Beowulf, a heroic poem of the eighth century, with a translation, notes, and appendix, by Thomas Arnold, M.A. London : Longmans, Green & Co., 1876. 8°, pp. xliii, 223.

Fourth English Translation. Prose.

Circumstances of Publication.

No edition of the text of *Beowulf* had appeared in England since the work of Thorpe [1], now twenty years

---

[1] See supra, p. 49.

old. The textual criticism of the Germans had, meanwhile, greatly advanced the interpretation of the poem. Grein's text of the poem had passed into a second, and Heyne's into a third, edition. There was an opportunity, therefore, for an improved English edition which should incorporate the results of German scholarship. This edition Mr. Thomas Arnold (1823–1900) undertook to supply.

Relation of the Parts.

The Introduction contained a new theory of the origin of the poem[1]. But the important part of the book was the text and translation. There is no glossary[2]. The notes are at the bottom of the page. Here glossarial, textual, and literary information is bundled together. There is a very inadequate bibliography in the Introduction.

Nature of the Translation.

The translation is a literal prose version, printed under the text. It resembles Kemble's work[3], rather than Thorpe's[4]. It eschews unwieldy compounds, and makes no attempt to acquire an archaic flavor. Supplied words are bracketed.

Criticism of the Text.

Arnold had access to the MS., and gave the most thorough description of it that had yet appeared. But, strangely enough, he did not make it the basis of his edition. He speaks of a 'partial collation' of the MS.,

---

[1] A theory which the author continued to regard as partially tenable. See *Notes on Beowulf* (London, 1898), p. 114.
[2] Contrast this with the editions of Heyne. See p. 64.
[3] See supra, p. 33.
[4] See supra, p. 49.

but this appears to have been nothing mroe than a transcription of certain fragmentary parts of the MS. One of these passages is printed in the Introduction, where it is referred to as an 'exact transcript'; yet, in collating it with the Zupitza *Autotypes*, I have found the following errors:—

> Line 2219[1], þeowes *for* þeofes.
> 2220, biorn *for* beorna.
> 2221, geweoldum *for* ge weoldum.
> 2223, b *for* þ.
> 2225, wea . . . *for* weal . . .
> 2226, inwlitode, inwatode *for* mwatide.

Of course the faded condition of the MS. offers some excuse for one or two of these errors, but, if we encounter mistakes in a short transcript professedly exact, what would have been the fate of the text had the entire MS. been collated?

Professor Garnett[2] has noted that Arnold's text was taken from Thorpe's, with some changes to suit the 1857 text of Grein. In order to test the accuracy of these statements I have made a collation of the texts of Arnold, Thorpe, and the MS. The list of errors in Thorpe's text, which I have mentioned in a discussion of that work[3], is repeated bodily in Arnold's. Yet there was no excuse at this time for the retention of many of these readings. Grundtvig[4] had corrected several of them as early as 1861 by his collation of the Thorkelin transcripts[5]; Heyne had got rid of them by collating Thorpe's work with Kemble's[6] and Grundtvig's. Arnold makes almost no

---

[1] The numbers are those of Wyatt's text; for Zupitza's and Arnold's add 1.
[2] See *Amer. Journal of Philol.* I. 1. 90.
[3] See supra, p. 51.
[4] See *Beowulfs Beorh*, and p. 22.
[5] See supra, p. 15.   [6] See supra, p. 33.

reference to the work of Heyne, and incorporates none of his emendations. He also overlooked Grein's 1867 text, which contained new readings and a glossary. Arnold himself did not emend the text in a single instance.

EXTRACT.

VIII.

Hunferth spake, the son of Ecglaf, who sat at the feet of the master of the Scyldings; he unbound the secret counsel of his malice. The expedition of Beowulf, the valiant mariner, was to him a great cause of offence; for that he allowed not that any other man on the earth should ever appropriate more deeds of fame under heaven than he himself. 'Art thou that Beowulf who strove against Breca in a swimming-match on the broad sea? where ye two for emulation explored the waves, and for foolish boasting ventured your lives in the deep water. Nor could any man, either friend or foe, warn you off from your perilous adventure. Then ye two rowed on the sea, where with your arms [outspread] ye covered the ocean-stream, measured the sea-ways, churned up [the water] with your hands, glided over the deep; the sea was tossing with waves, the icy wintry sea. Ye two toiled for seven nights in the watery realm; he overcame thee in the match, he had more strength. Then, at dawn of morn, the sea cast him up on [the coast of] the Heathoreamas; thence he, dear in the sight of his people, sought his loved native soil, the land of the Brondings, the fair safe burgh where he was the owner of folk, burgh, and precious jewels.'—Pages 37, 38.

Criticism of the Translation.

The translation is literal, and its value is therefore in direct ratio to the value of the text, which has been discussed above.

BOTKINE'S TRANSLATION

Beowulf, Épopée Anglo-Saxonne. Traduite en français, pour la première fois, d'après le texte original par L. Botkine, Membre de la Société Nationale havraise d'Études diverses. Havre: Lepelletier, 1877. 8°, pp. 108.
First French Translation. Prose.

Old English Studies in France.

The only attention that *Beowulf* had received in France prior to this time was in the work of Sandras, *De Carminibus Cædmoni adiudicatis*[1]. Other scholars, if they devoted themselves to English at all, studied chiefly the later periods of the literature[2]. In 1867 the author of the article on *Beowulf* in Larousse's Dictionary could say, ' Le poème n'est pas connu en France.' In 1876 Botkine published a historical and critical analysis of the poem[3]. This was the first scholarly attention that the poem received in France. In the following year Botkine's translation appeared.

France has added nothing to our knowledge of *Beowulf*; there has never been another translation, nor even a reprint of Botkine's. There has been no further scholarly work done on the poem ; and the principal literary notices of it, such as Taine's and Jusserand's, have been notoriously unsympathetic. The genius of Old English poetry is at the furthest possible remove from that of the French.

Aim of the Translation.

It will be made evident in the section that follows on the nature of Botkine's translation that his work could never

---

[1] See infra, p. 123.
[2] Save Michel. An account of his work may be found in Wülker's *Grundriss*, § 102.
[3] *Analyse historique et géographique.* Paris, Leroux, 1876.

have been intended for scholars. Had it been so intended, the translator would have rendered more literally. His introduction [1] proves that the book was addressed to the general reader rather than the student of Old English. The Introduction deals with the nature of Old English poetry, and makes historical and critical remarks on the *Beowulf*. There are occasional notes explanatory of the text.

In his critical work the author is chiefly indebted to Grein [2] and Heyne [3].

Nature of the Translation.

The translation, which is in prose, is characterized, as the author himself admits, by extreme freedom and occasional omission of words and phrases. The author's defence of these may be given here :—

' Je crois devoir me disculper, en présentant cette première traduction française de Beowulf, du double reproche qui pourrait m'être adressé d'avoir supprimé des passages du poëme et de n'en avoir pas suffisamment respecté la lettre. D'abord je dois dire que les passages que j'ai supprimés (il y en a fort peu) sont ou très obscurs ou d'une superfluité choquante. Ensuite, il m'a semblé qu'en donnant une certaine liberté à ma traduction et en évitant autant que possible d'y mettre les redites et les périphrases de l'original anglo-saxon, je la rendrais meilleure et plus conforme à l'esprit véritable de l'œuvre. Est-ce sacrifier du reste la fidélité d'une traduction que d'épargner au public la lecture de détails le plus souvent bizarres et inintelligibles ? N'est-il pas plus logique d'en finir de suite avec des artifices poétiques inconnus à nos littératures modernes, plutôt que de vouloir s'escrimer en vain à les reproduire en français ? Et alors même qu'on poursuivrait jusqu'au bout une tâche si ingrate, pourrait-on se flatter en fin de compte d'avoir conservé au poëme son cachet si indiscutable d'originalité ? Non certes.'—Avertissement, p. 3.

' Il ne faut pas oublier que, la langue française différant complète-

---

[1] p. 4.   [2] See supra, p. 55.
        [3] See supra, p. 63.

ment par ses racines de l'anglo-saxon, il ne m'a pas été permis d'éluder les difficultés de l'original comme on a pu le faire parfois en anglais et en allemand.'—Note, p. 4.

It has been customary, in speaking of the work of M. Botkine, to call attention to the numerous omissions. This is misleading. The passages which the translator has omitted are not the obscure episodes or the long digressions, but the metaphors, the parenthetical phrases, and especially kennings and similar appositives.

For example, the original has :—

> þær æt hȳde stōd hringed-stefna
> īsig ond ūt-fūs. (l. 32 f.)

which Botkine renders :—

> Dans la porte se trouvait une barque bien équipée. (p. 29.)

The principal passages which Botkine omits entirely are : 1002 b–1008 a ; 1057 b–1062 ; 1263–1276 ; 1679–1686.

Text Used.

The author seems to have been well acquainted with the scholarly work done on *Beowulf* up to his time. He mentions in his Notes the interpretations of Grein, Grundtvig[1], Ettmüller[2], Thorpe[3], and Kemble[4]. He appears to follow, in general, the text of Heyne, not, however, invariably.

EXTRACT.

IX.

Hunferth, fils d'Ecglaf, qui était assis aux pieds du prince des Scyldingas, parla ainsi (l'expédition de Beowulf[5] le remplissait de chagrin, parce qu'il ne voulait pas convenir qu'aucun homme[6] eût plus de gloire[7] que lui-même) :

'N'es-tu pas le Beowulf qui essaya ses forces à la nage sur la

---

[1] See supra, p. 22.
[3] See supra, p. 49.
[5] Omits mōdges mere-faran.
[7] Omits under heofonum.

[2] See supra, p. 37.
[4] See supra, p. 33.
[6] Omits middan-geardes.

mer immense avec Breca quand, par bravade, vous avez tenté les flots
et que vous avez follement hasardé votre vie dans l'eau profonde ?
Aucun homme, qu'il fût ami ou ennemi, ne put vous empêcher d'entre-
prendre ce triste voyage.—Vous avez nagé alors sur la mer [1], vous
avez suivi les sentiers de l'océan. L'hiver agitait les vagues [2]. Vous
êtes restés en détresse pendant sept nuits sous la puissance des flots,
mais il t'a vaincu dans la joûte parce qu'il avait plus de force que toi.
Le matin, le flot le porta sur Heatho-ræmas et il alla visiter sa chère
patrie [3] le pays des Brondingas, où il possédait le peuple, une ville et
des trésors. Le fils de Beanstan accomplit entièrement la promesse
qu'il t'avait faite.'

Criticism of the Extract and Translation.

If the translation is compared with the text, the reader
will be struck by the characteristic beauty of the words
omitted. We may agree with the translator regarding the
difficulty of rendering compound and kenning into French,
and yet the very absence of an attempt to do this
jeopardizes the value of the translation more than the
omission of many episodes, for it brings it dangerously near
to paraphrase. 'Vous avez nagé alors sur la mer, vous
avez suivi les sentiers de l'océan,' cannot possibly be called
a translation of—

> þā git on sund rēon ;
> þǣr git ēagor-strēam   earmum þehton,
> mǣton mere-strǣta, mundum brugdon,
> glidon ofer gār-secg.   ll. 512, ff.

A part of the story has been thrown away with the adjectives. The force and beauty of the passage are gone.

But there is another danger in this paraphrastic method.
In omitting words and phrases, the translator will often
misinterpret his original. This is especially true of
Botkine's work in the obscure episodes where he wishes
to make the meaning perfectly clear. In attempting to
simplify the Old English, he departs from the original

---

[1] Omits lines 513–515 [a].   [2] Omits wintrys wylum.
[3] Omits lēof his lēodum.

sense. Instances of this may be brought forward from the Finn episode:

> Folcwaldan sunu
> dōgra gehwylce Dene weorþode,
> Hengestes hēap hringum wenede,
> efne swā swīðe sinc-gestrēonum
> fættan goldes, swā hē Frēsena cyn
> on bēor-sele byldan wolde.   ll. 1089 ff.

The idea is misinterpreted in Botkine's—

Le fils de Folcwalda (stipulait qu'il) leur ferait chaque jour une distribution de trésors. (p. 50.)

Again, at line 1117 it is said of the lady—

> earme on eaxle   ides gnornode,

meaning that the lady stood by the body (shoulder) of the corpse as it lay on the pyre. Botkine makes of this—

'Elle poussait des lamentations en s'appuyant sur le bras de son fils.' (p. 50.)

The rendering is not without its amusing features, chiefly illustrations of the inability of the French language to accommodate itself to typically Germanic expressions. Thus when Hrothgar says what is the equivalent of 'Thanks be to God for this blessed sight,' Botkine puts into his mouth the words: 'Que le Tout-Puissant reçoive mes profonds remercîments pour ce spectacle!'—which might have been taken from a diplomatic note.

LUMSDEN'S TRANSLATION

Beowulf, an Old English Poem, translated into Modern Rhymes, by Lieut.-Colonel H. W. Lumsden[1]. London: C. Kegan Paul & Co., 1881. 8°, pp. xx, 114.

[1] Col. Lumsden's translation of the Battle of Maldon, *Macmillan's Magazine*, 55: 371, has been generally admired.

Beowulf, an Old English Poem, translated into Modern Rhymes, by Lieut.-Colonel H. W. Lumsden, late Royal Artillery. Second edition, revised and corrected. London: Kegan Paul, Trench and Co., 1883. 8°, pp. xxx, 179.

Fifth English Translation.   Ballad Measures.

Differences between the two Editions, and Indebtedness to Preceding Scholars.

In the first edition of the translation a number of passages were omitted.   Some of these omissions were owing to corrupt text, some to extreme obscurity of the original, and some merely to the fact that the original was deemed uninteresting.   The principal omissions were: 83–86; 767–770; 1724–1758; 1931–1963; 2061–2062; 2214–2231; 2475; 2930–2932; 3150–3156.   These passages were inserted in the second edition.

'In this edition I have endeavoured to remove some of the blunders which disfigured its predecessor. . . . Some parts have been entirely rewritten, and the passages formerly omitted . . . have been inserted. . . . A few notes have been added; and the introduction has been materially altered and, I hope, improved.'—Preface to the Second Edition, p. v.

Aim and Nature of the Translation.

Lumsden's desire was to produce a readable version of the poem.   Thus his work resembles that of Wackerbarth[1]; and, like Wackerbarth, he couched his translation in ballad measures.   Lumsden does not vary his measure, but preserves the iambic heptameter throughout.   His lines rime in couplets.

No attempt is made to preserve alliteration or archaic diction.

The Introduction and Notes contain popular expositions of the work of preceding scholars.   Several of the Notes are original and well worth while (see Notes A, C, G, M).

[1] See supra, p. 45.

Texts Used.

The translation is based on Grein's text of 1857[1] and Arnold's text (1876)[2]. Garnett has shown[3] that Lumsden ignored the 1867 text of Grein and the editions of Heyne. These defects were remedied to some extent in the second edition. Lumsden himself never emends the text.

EXTRACT[4].

IV. HUNFERD AND BEOWULF.

Hunferd the son of Ecglaf spoke—at Hrothgar's feet sat he—
And thus let loose his secret grudge; (for much did him displease
The coming of Beowulf now—bold sailor o'er the seas.
To none on earth would he allow a greater fame 'mong men
Beneath the heavens than his): 'Art thou the same Beowulf then,
Who swam a match with Breca once upon the waters wide,
When ye vainglorious searched the waves, and risked your lives for
    pride
Upon the deep? Nor hinder you could any friend or foe
From that sad venture. Then ye twain did on the waters row;
Ye stretched your arms upon the flood; the sea-ways ye did mete; 10
O'er billows glided—with your hands them tossed—though fiercely
    beat
The rolling tides and wintry waves! Seven nights long toilèd ye
In waters' might; but Breca won—he stronger was than thee!
And to the Hathoræms at morn washed shoreward by the flood,
Thence his loved native land he sought—the Brondings' country
    good,
And stronghold fair, where he was lord of folk and burg and rings.
Right well 'gainst thee his vaunt he kept.

Criticism of the Translation.

The extract illustrates the paraphrastic nature of parts of the translation. Lumsden frequently seems to feel it necessary to read a meaning into the obscure lines and

[1] See supra, p. 56. [2] See supra, p. 72.
[3] See *American Journal of Philology*, ii. p. 355.
[4] From the second edition.

passages that do not easily lend themselves to translation ;
cf. lines 11, 12.   At line 2258 Lumsden translates :—

> The mail that bite of sword
> O'er clashing shield in fight withstood must follow its dead lord.
> Never again shall corselet ring as help the warriors bear
> To comrades far.

The Old English from which this passage is taken
reads :—

> ge swylce sēo here-pād,   sīo æt hilde gebād
> ofer borda gebræc   bite īrena,
> brosnað æfter beorne ;   ne mæg byrnan hring   2260
> æfter wīg-fruman   wīde fēran
> hæleðum be healfe.

The passage is certainly obscure, and the readings are not
all undoubted, but the words can never be tortured into
meaning what Lumsden tries to make them mean.

But it would be manifestly unfair to judge a translation
addressed to the general reader merely by scholarly tests.
The work must make its appeal as a literary rendering.

The propriety of adopting a ballad measure may be
questioned.   Probably no measure could be found more
unlike the Old English lines.   Moreover, by reason of its
long association with purely popular poetry, it constantly
suggests the commonplace and the trivial.   But above all,
it is reminiscent of a medievalism wholly different from
that of *Beowulf*.

The saving grace of the ballad measure is its readableness.   It is rather effective in passages not too dignified,
calling for action.   But in passages of elevation the line is
found wanting :—

They mourned their king and chanted dirge, and much of him they
    said ;
His worthiness they praised, and judged his deeds with tender dread.

But, like Wackerbarth's, Lumsden's translation had the
advantage of being readable.

GARNETT'S TRANSLATION

Beowun : An Anglo-Saxon Poem, and the Fight at Finnsburg, translated by James M. Garnett, M.A., LL.D., Boston, U.S.A. : published by Ginn, Heath, & Co., 1882. 8°, pp. xl, 107.
Second Edition, Ginn, Heath, & Co., 1885.   8°, pp. xlvi, 110.
Third Edition, Ginn & Co., 1892.   Reprinted 1899. 8°, pp. liii, 110.
Fourth Edition, 1900.
Sixth English Translation.   Imitative Measures.

Differences between the Editions.

In the second edition the translation was collated with the Grein-Wülker text, and wherever necessary, with the Zupitza *Autotypes*.   Additions were made to the bibliography :—

‘ I have revised certain passages with a view to greater accuracy, but I have not changed the plan of the work, for that would have necessitated the re-writing of the whole translation.’—Preface to the second edition.

The third and fourth editions are simple reprints, with some additions to the bibliography.

Circumstances of Publication.

As has been pointed out above in the sections on Arnold [1] and Lumsden [2], no satisfactory literal translation of *Beowulf* existed in English.   Furthermore, an American translation had never appeared.   It was with a view to presenting the latest German interpretations of the poem

[1] See supra, p. 71.   [2] See supra, p. 79.

that Garnett prepared his literal version of the poem. The original draft of the translation was made at St. John's College, Md., in the session of 1878–79.—Preface to first edition.

Texts Used.

The translation is based on Grein's text of 1867. Notes are added showing the variants from Heyne's text of 1879. In the second edition notes are added showing the variants from the Grein-Wülker text of 1883.

Method of Translation.

The translation is intended for 'the general reader' and for the 'aid of students of the poem.'—Preface to second edition.

The translation is a literal line-for-line version. Of this feature of his work Professor Garnett says :—

'This involves naturally much inversion and occasional obscurity, and lacks smoothness ; but it seemed to me to give the general reader a better idea of the poem than a mere prose translation would do, in addition to the advantage of literalness. While it would have been easy, by means of periphrasis and freer translation, to mend some of the defects chargeable to the line-for-line form, the translation would have lacked literalness, which I regarded as the most important object.'—Preface to the first edition.

Nature of the Verse-form.

In respect to the rhythmical form, I have endeavored to preserve two accents to each half-line, with cæsura, and while not seeking alliteration, have employed it purposely wherever it readily presented itself. I considered that it mattered little whether the feet were iambi or trochees, anapæsts or dactyls, the preservation of the two accents being the main point, and have freely made use of all the usual licences in Early English verse. ... To attain this point I have sometimes found it necessary to place unemphatic words in accented positions, and words usually accented in unaccented ones, which licence can also be found in Early English verse. ... While the reader of modern English verse may sometimes be offended by the ruggedness of the rhythm, it is hoped that the Anglo-Saxon scholar will make allowances for the difficulty of reproducing, even approximately, the rhythm of the original. The reproduction of the sense as closely as possible had to be kept constantly in view, even to the detriment of the smoothness of the rhythm.'—Preface to the first edition.

EXTRACT.
III.

Hunferth's taunt.   The swimming-match with Breca.
Joy in Heorot.

IX. Hunferth then spoke, the son of Ecglaf,
500 Who at the feet sat of the lord of the Scyldings,
Unloosed his war-secret (was the coming of Beowulf,
The proud sea-farer, to him mickle grief,
For that he granted not that any man else
Ever more honor of this mid-earth
505 Should gain under heavens than he himself):
'Art thou that Beowulf who strove with Breca
On the broad sea in swimming-match,
When ye two for pride the billows tried
And for vain boasting in the deep water
510 Riskéd your lives. You two no man,
Nor friend nor foe, might then dissuade
From sorrowful venture, when ye on the sea swam,
When ye the sea-waves with your arms covered,
Measured the sea-ways, struck with your hands,
515 Glided o'er ocean; with its great billows
Welled up winter's flood. In the power of the waters
Ye seven nights strove : he in swimming thee conquered,
He had greater might. Then him in the morning
On the Heathoremes' land the ocean bore up,
520 Whence he did seek his pleasant home,
Dear to his people, the land of the Brondings
His fair strong city, where he had people,
A city and rings. All his boast against thee
The son of Beanstan truly fulfilled.'

Criticism of the Translation.

The translation, in its revised form, is throughout a faithful version of the original text. The fault of Garnett's translation is the fault of all merely literal translations—inadequacy to render fully the content of the original. The rendering may be word for word, but it will not be idea for idea. Examples of this inadequacy may be given from the printed extract. 'Grief' in line 502 is a very insufficient rendering of *æf-þunca*, a unique word which suggests at once vexation, mortification, and jealousy. Had the poet simply meant to express the notion of *grief*, he would have used *sorh*, *cearu*, or some other common word. In line 508 'pride' hardly gives full expression to the idea of *wlence*, which signifies not only *pride*, but *vain pride, of empty end*. In line 517 'conquered' is insufficient as a translation of *oferflāt*, which means to *overcome in swimming, to outswim*.

Examples of this sort can be brought forward from any part of the poem. At line 2544 Garnett translates—

> Struggles of battle when warriors contended,

a translation of—

> Gūða . . . þonne hnitan fēðan

Here 'hnitan fēðan' refers to the swift clash in battle of two armed hosts, a notion which is ill borne out by the distributive 'warriors' and the vague 'contended.'

At line 2598 we find—

> they to wood went

for

> hȳ on holt bugon,

which, whatever be the meaning of 'bugon,' is surely a misleading translation.

The nature of the verse has been sufficiently illustrated by the quotations from the author's preface. It would seem from the way in which the measure is used that it was a kind of second thought, incident upon the use of a line-for-line translation. It is hard to read the lines as anything but prose, and, if they appeared in any other form upon the page, it is to be questioned whether any one would have guessed that they were intended to be imitative.

Reception of Garnett's Translation.

Garnett's volume had a flattering reception. The book received long and respectful reviews from the Germans. Professor Child and Henry Sweet expressed their approbation. The book has passed through four editions. This cordial welcome has been due in large measure to the increasing attention given the poem in American colleges and secondary schools. Being strictly literal, the book has been of value as a means of interpreting the poem.

GRION'S TRANSLATION

Beovulf, poema epico anglosassone del vii secolo, tradotto e illustrato dal Dott. Cav. Giusto Grion, Socio Ordinario.

In Atti della Reale Accademia Lucchese di Scienze, Lettere ed Arti. Tomo XXII. Lucca: Tipografia Giusti, 1883. 8°, pp. 197–379.

First Italian Translation. Imitative Measures.

Contents.

Full discussions of (1) Mito; (2) Storia; (3) Letteratura. The latter is a fairly complete bibliography of what had been done on *Beowulf* up to this time.

Author's Preliminary Remarks.

' Il poema consiste di 3183 versi fra cui alcuni in frammenti che noi abbiamo cercato di completare senza alterare lettera del testo. Una mano recente lo ha diviso in 43 canti, detti in ags. fitte ; ne notiamo il numero anche nella versione. I versi che il Müllenhoff reputa inter-polati, sono disposti in linee rientranti ; quelli attributi ad A portano di più questa lettera nella versione nostra interlineare, che segue la parola del testo in maniera da mantenervi anche la sintassi, e si che nessuna parola d'un verso prenda posto in un' altra riga. Le parentesi quadre [ ] segnano nel testo riempiture di lacune. Nella versione sono queste segnate per lettere corsive.'—Prefazione, p. 251.

Texts Used.

The translator makes use of all the texts and commen-taries that had appeared up to his time, and even goes so far as to emend the text for himself (cf. lines 65, 665, 1107, 2561, 3150).

The Notes are rather full. They are sometimes merely explanatory ; sometimes there are discussions of the MS. readings, of proposed emendations, of history, myth, &c.

Method of Translation.

The translation is literal ; the medium an imitative measure of four principal stresses, varied occasionally by the expanded line. The diction is simple.

EXTRACT.

VIII.

Hunferd disse, il nato di Eclaf,
500 che a' piedi sedea del prence de' Schildinghi,
     sbrigliò accenti di contesta—eragli la gita di Beóvulf,
     del coraggioso navigatore, molto a fastidio,
     perchè non amava, che un altro uomo
     vieppiù di gloria nell' orbe di mezzo
505 avesse sotto il cielo che lui stesso—:
     ' Sei tu quel Beóvulf, che con Breca nuotò

nel vasto pelago per gara marina,
quando voi per baldanza l'acque provaste,
e per pazzo vanto nel profondo sale
510 la vita arrischiaste? nè voi uomo alcuno,
nè caro nè discaro, distorre potè
dalla penosa andata, quando remigaste nell' alto,
la corrente dell' oceano colle braccia coprendo
misuraste le strade del mare, colle mani batteste,
515 e scivolaste sopra l'astato. Nelle onde del ghebbo
vagavano i cavalloni d'inverno: voi nel tenere dell' acqua
sette notti appenàstevi. Egli nel nuoto ti superò,
ebbe più forza. E al tempo mattutino lo
portò suso il flutto verso la marittima Ramia
520 donde ei cercò la dolce patria,
cara a sue genti, la terra dei Brondinghi,
il vago castel tranquillo, ov' egli popolo avea,
rocche e gioie. Il vanto intero contro te
il figlio di Beanstan in verità mantenne.'

Criticism of the Translation.

The present writer cannot attempt a literary criticism of
the translation.

In purpose and method this version may be compared
with that of Kemble[1] and of Schaldemose[2]. In each case
the translator was introducing the poem to a foreign public,
and it was therefore well that the translation should be
literal in order that it might assist in the interpretation of
the original. There has been no further work done on the
poem in Italy[3].

While the verse is not strictly imitative in the sense that
it preserves exactly the Old English system of versification,
it aims to maintain the general movement of the original
lines. The four stresses are kept, save where a fifth is used
to avoid monotony. These 'expanded lines' are much
commoner in the Italian than in the Old English.

[1] See supra, p. 33.   [2] See supra, p. 41.
[3] Of a work by G. Schuhmann, mentioned by Wülker in his *Grundriss*,
§ 209, I can ascertain nothing.

WICKBERG'S TRANSLATION

Beowulf, en fornengelsk hjeltedikt, öfversatt af Rudolf Wickberg. Westervik, C. O. Ekblad & Comp., 1889. 4°, pp. 48, double columns.

First Swedish Translation. Imitative Measures.

Aim of the Volume.

The translator begins his introduction with a discussion of the importance of *Beowulf* as a historical document. For this reason he is especially interested in the episodes :—

'This important historical interest may then explain the reason for translating the poem into Swedish, and also serve as an excuse for the fact that in the translation the poetic form has not been considered of first importance.'—Inledning, p. 3.

Nature of the Translation.

'In the translation I have endeavored to make the language readable and modern. A translation out of an ancient tongue ought never to strive after archaic flavor in point of words and expressions. Since the poet wrote in the language of his day, the translation ought also to use contemporary language. . . . I have tried to follow the original faithfully, but not slavishly. For the sake of clearness the half-lines have often been transposed . . . The rhythm is still more irregular than the Old English. Alliteration has generally been avoided.'—Inledning, p. 6.

Texts Used.

The author constructs his own text. He explains (p. 6) that he has in general taken the MS. as the basis of his text. He has emended by making those changes which 'seemed most necessary or most probable.' In places where this departure from the MS. has been made, he italicizes the words of his translation.

EXTRACT.

8.

Ecglafs son Hunferd talade ;
Vid Scyldingafurstens fötter satt han,
Löste stridsrunan—den modige sjöfaranden
Beovulfs resa förtröt honom mycket,
Förty han unnade ej, att någon annan man
Under himlen skulle någonsin vinna
Större ära på jorden än han sjelf— :
' Är du den Beovulf, som mätte sig med Breca
I kappsimning öfver det vida hafvet,
Der I öfvermodigt pröfvaden vågorna
Och för djerft skryt vågaden lifvet
I det djupa vattnet ? Ej kunde någon man,
Ljuf eller led, förmå eder att afstå
Från den sorgfulla färden. Sedan summen I i hafvet,
Der I med armarna famnaden hafsströmmen,
Mätten hafsvågorna, svängden händerna,
Gleden öfver hafsytan ; vintersvallet
Sjöd i vågorna. I sträfvaden sju nätter
I hafvets våld ; han öfvervann dig i simning,
Hade större styrka. Sedan vid morgontiden
Bar hafvet upp honom till de krigiska rämerna.
Derifrån uppsökte han, dyr för de sina,
Sitt kära odal i brondingarnes land,
Den fagra fridsborgen, der han hade folk,
Berg och ringar. Hela sitt vad med dig
Fullgjorde noga Beanstans son.'

EARLE'S TRANSLATION

The Deeds of Beowulf, an English Epic of the Eighth
Century, done into Modern Prose, with an Introduction and
Notes by John Earle, M.A., rector of Swanswick, Rawlin-
sonian Professor of Anglo-Saxon in the University of Oxford.
At the Clarendon Press, 1892 (February). 8°, pp. c, 203.
Seventh English Translation. Prose.

Circumstances of Publication.

Sixteen years had elapsed since the publication of a scholarly translation in England—for Lumsden's[1] can hardly be said to count as such. In the meantime Heyne's text[2] had passed into a fifth edition (1888); Wülker's revision of Grein's *Bibliothek* had appeared with a new text of *Beowulf* (1881); Zupitza's *Autotypes* of the MS. had appeared 1882, making it possible to ascertain exactly what was in the original text of the poem ; the studies of Sievers[3], Cosijn[4], Kluge[5], and Bugge[6] had been published, containing masterly discussions of text revision. Some of these materials had been used by Garnett in his translation, but the majority of them were of later date.

Aim of the Translation.

Nothing is said in the introduction respecting the aim of the translation ; but it is evident from the Notes that the purpose was twofold—to present the latest interpretation of the text, and to afford a literary version of the poem.

Texts Used.

' This translation was originally made from the Fourth Edition of Moritz Heyne's text. His Fifth Edition came out in 1888, and I think I have used it enough to become acquainted with all the changes that Dr. Adolf Socin, the new editor, has introduced. Where they have appeared to me to be improvements, I have modified my translation accordingly.'—Preface.

But the translator does not depend slavishly upon his text. He frequently uses emendations suggested by the scholars mentioned above, especially those of Professor

---

[1] See supra, p. 79.   [2] See supra, p. 64.
[3] Paul und Braune's *Beiträge*, XI, 328 ; Ang. XIV, 133.
[4] *Beiträge*, VIII, 568 ; *Aanteekeningen*, Leiden 1891.
[5] *Beiträge*, IX, 187 ; VIII, 532.
[6] *Beiträge*, XI, 1 ; *Studien über das Beowulfsepos.*

Sophus Bugge in *Studien über das Beowulfsepos* [1]; see lines 457, 871, 900, 926, 1875, 2275.

The Introduction presents a new theory of the origin of the poem. The notes are especially interesting because of the large body of quotations cited for literary comparison and for the light they throw on Old Germanic and medieval customs.

EXTRACT.

VIII.

Unferth the king's orator is jealous. He baits the young adventurer, and in a scoffing speech dares him to a night-watch for Grendel. Beowulf is angered, and thus he is drawn out to boast of his youthful feats.

Unferth made a speech, Ecglaf's son ; he who sate at the feet of the Scyldings' lord, broached a quarrelsome theme—the adventure of Beowulf the high-souled voyager was great despite to him, because he grudged that any other man should ever in the world achieve more exploits under heaven than he himself:—'Art thou *that* Beowulf, he who strove with Breca on open sea in swimming-match, where ye twain out of bravado explored the floods, and foolhardily in deep water jeoparded your lives? nor could any man, friend or foe, turn the pair of you from the dismal adventure! What time ye twain plied in swimming, where ye twain covered with your arms the awful stream, meted the sea-streets, buffeted with hands, shot over ocean ; the deep boiled with waves, a wintry surge. Ye twain in the realm of waters toiled a se'nnight ; he at swimming outvied thee, had greater force. Then in morning hour the swell cast him ashore on the Heathoram people, whence he made for his own patrimony, dear to his Leeds he made for the land of the Brondings, a fair stronghold, where he was lord of folk, of city, and of rings. All his boast to thee-ward, Beanstan's son soothly fulfilled. Wherefore I anticipate for thee worse luck—though thou wert everywhere doughty in battle-shocks, in grim war-tug—if thou darest bide in Grendel's way a night-long space.'

Criticism of the Translation.

As a whole, the translation may fairly be called faithful. The emendations from which Professor Earle sometimes

[1] *Beiträge*, XI, 1 ff.

renders are always carefully chosen, and the discussions of obscure lines in the poem are of real scholarly interest. But this is not always true of the simpler passages of the poem. These are often strained to make them square with the translator's personal notions. Thus, at line 1723, Earle reads for

> *Ic þis gid be þē āwraec*
> It is about thee . . . that I have told this tale,

adding in a note, '(In this passage) the living poet steps forward out of his Hrothgar, and turns his eyes to the prince for whom he made it up' (p. 168). Now this is nothing more than an attempt on the part of the translator to wring from the Old English lines some scrap of proof for the peculiar theory that he holds of the origin of the poem.

Similarly, he often reads into a single word more than it can possibly bear. At line 371 he translates—

> *Hrothgar, helm Scyldinga,*
> Hrothgar, crown of Scyldings.

But 'crown' is an impossible rendering of 'helm,' which is here used figuratively to denote the idea of protection [1], rather than the idea of the crowning glory of kingship. Further, in the same passage, 375-6, *heard eafora* (bold son), is wrenched into meaning 'grown-up son.' These are but two examples of what is common throughout the translation.

Diction.

The archaic style used by Professor Earle cannot be regarded as highly felicitous, since it mixes the diction of various ages. Here are Old English archaisms like

---

[1] See the glossaries of Grein and Wyatt.

'Leeds' and 'burnie'; here are expressions like 'escheat,' 'page' (attendant), 'emprize,' 'bombard' (drinking-vessel), 'chivalry.' Here are such specialized words as 'harpoon,' 'belligerent,' 'pocket-money,' and combinations like 'battailous grip'; while throughout the entire translation are scattered modern colloquialisms like 'boss' (master), 'tussle,' 'war-tug.'

The reason for these anomalies is evident—the translator wishes to imitate the remoteness of the original style. The style is certainly remote—at times almost as remote from the language of to-day as is the style of *Beowulf* itself.

J. L. HALL'S TRANSLATION

Beowulf, an Anglo-Saxon Epic Poem, translated by John Lesslie Hall. Boston: D. C. Heath and Co., 1892 (May 7). Reprinted 1900. 8°, pp. xviii, 110.

Eighth English Translation. Imitative Measures.

Circumstances of Publication.

Presented to the Philosophical Faculty of Johns Hopkins University in candidacy for the degree of Doctor of Philosophy by John Lesslie Hall, late Professor in the college of William and Mary.

Aim of the Translation.

'The work is addressed to two classes of readers. . . . The Anglo-Saxon scholar he [the translator] hopes to please by adhering faithfully to the original. The student of English literature he aims to interest by giving him, in modern garb, the most ancient epic of our race.'—Preface, vii.

Nature of the Translation.

The translation is in imitative measures and in archaic style.

'The effort has been made to give a decided flavor of archaism to the translation. All words not in keeping with the spirit of the poem have been avoided. Again, though many archaic words have been used, there are none, it is believed, which are not found in standard modern poetry. . . .

'The measure used in the present translation is believed to be as near a reproduction of the original as modern English affords. . . . The four stresses of the Anglo-Saxon verse are retained, and as much thesis and anacrusis is allowed as is consistent with a regular cadence. Alliteration has been used to a large extent ; but it was thought that modern ears would hardly tolerate it in every line. End-rhyme has been used occasionally ; internal rhyme, sporadically. . . .

'What Gummere calls the "rime-giver" has been studiously kept ; viz., the first accented syllable in the second half-verse always carries the alliteration ; and the last accented syllable alliterates only sporadically. . . .

'No two accented syllables have been brought together, except occasionally after a cæsural pause. . . . Or, scientifically speaking, Sievers's C type has been avoided as not consonant with the plan of translation.'—Preface, viii, ix.

Text.

'The Heyne-Socin text and glossary have been closely followed. Occasionally a deviation has been made. . . . Once in a while . . . (the translator) has added a conjecture of his own to the emendations quoted from the criticisms of other students of the poem.'—Preface, vii.

The footnotes which contain the conjectural readings are interesting, and in one or two cases valuable additions to the suggested emendations (cf. p. 15 ; p. 103, note 3).

EXTRACT.

IX.

UNFERTH TAUNTS BEOWULF.

Unferth spoke up, Ecglaf his son,
Who sat at the feet of the lord of the Scyldings,
Opened the jousting (the journey of Beowulf,
Sea-farer doughty, gave sorrow to Unferth
5 And greatest chagrin, too, for granted he never
That any man else on earth should attain to,
Gain under heaven, more glory than he):
'Art thou that Beowulf with Breca did struggle,
On the wide sea-currents at swimming contended,
10 Where to humor your pride the ocean ye tried,
From vainest vaunting adventured your bodies
In care of the waters? And no one was able
Nor lief nor loth one, in the least to dissuade you
Your difficult voyage; then ye ventured a-swimming,
15 Where your arms outstretching the streams ye did
    cover,
The mere-ways measured, mixing and stirring them,
Glided the ocean; angry the waves were,
With the weltering of winter. In the water's posses-
    sion,
Ye toiled for a seven-night; he at swimming outdid
    thee,
20 In strength excelled thee. Then early at morning
On the Heathoremes' shore the holm-currents tossed
    him,
Sought he thenceward the home of his fathers,
Beloved of his liegemen, the land of the Brondings,
The peace-castle pleasant, where a people he wielded
25 Had borough and jewels. The pledge that he made
    thee
The son of Beanstan hath soothly accomplished
Then I ween thou wilt find thee less fortunate issue,
Though ever triumphant in onset of battle,
A grim grappling, if Grendel thou darest
30 For the space of a night near-by to wait for!

G

Marginal glosses:

Unferth, a thane of Hrothgar, is jealous of Beowulf, and undertakes to twit him.

Did you take part in a swimming-match with Breca?

'Twas mere folly that actuated you both to risk your lives on the ocean.

Breca outdid you entirely. Much more will Grendel outdo you, if you vie with him in prowess.

Criticism of the Translation.

The translation is faithful, but not literal. The chief difference, for example, between this and the translation by Garnett is that Hall makes an attempt to preserve the poetic value of the Old English words. He is never satisfied with the dictionary equivalent of an Old English expression. Thus, in the extract given above, 'from vainest vaunting' is given as a translation of *dol-gilpe*— a great improvement over Garnett's rendering, 'for pride.' Similarly, 'mixing and stirring' is given as a translation of *mundum brugdon*. This method often leads the translator some distance, perhaps too great a distance, from the Old English. The following may serve as examples of the heightened color that Hall gives to the Old English forms :—

548, 'the north-wind whistled, fierce in our faces,' for *norþan wind heaðo-grim ondhwearf.*

557, 'my obedient blade,' for *hilde-bille.*

568, 'foam-dashing currents,' for *brontne ford.*

587, 'with cold-hearted cruelty thou killedst thy brothers,' for *ðū þīnum brōðrum tō banan wurde.*

606, 'the sun in its ether robes,' for *sunne swegl-wered.*

838, 'in the mist of the morning,' for *on morgen.*

1311, 'As day was dawning in the dusk of the morning,' for *ǣr-dæge.*

Perhaps these paraphrastic renderings are what Dr. Hall is referring to when he says in his preface, regarding the nature of the translation, 'Occasionally some loss has been sustained; but, on the other hand, a gain has here and there been made.

As for the archaism, that is well enough for those who like it. It is never so strange as that of Earle, or the marvelous diction of William Morris. But it is not, therefore, dignified or clear. How much dignity and clarity a translator has a right to introduce into his rendering is a matter of opinion. Mr. Hall was quite conscious of what he was doing, and doubtless regarded his diction as well suited to convey the original Beowulf spirit. The chief criticism of the verse is that it is often not verse at all. Many passages are indistinguishable from prose. This is a stricture that cannot be passed on the Old English, nor on the best modern imitations of it.

> The atheling of Geatmen uttered these words and
> Heroic did hasten.—Page 51, line 19.
> In war 'neath the water the work with great pains I
> Performed.—Page 57, line 6.
> Gave me willingly to see on the wall a
> Heavy old hand-sword.—Page 57, line 11.
> The man was so dear that he failed to suppress the
> Emotions that moved him.—Page 64, line 59.

There might be an excuse for some of this freedom in blank verse, but in measures imitative of the Old English it is utterly out of place. There is always a pause at the end of a line in Old English; run-on lines are uncommon. There is not an example in *Beowulf* of an ending so light as the ' or ' a ' in the verses quoted above.

HOFFMANN'S TRANSLATION

Beówulf. Aeltestes deutsches Heldengedicht. Aus dem Angelsächsischen übertragen von P. Hoffmann. Züllichau. Verlag von Herm. Liebich (1893?). 8°, pp. iii, 183.

*Zweite Ausgabe, Hannover, Schaper, 1900.

Sixth German Translation. Nibelungen Measures.

The Translator.

In *Minerva* (1902), P. Hoffmann is recorded as ' Ord. Professor' of Philosophy and Pedagogy at Gent.

Aim of the Volume.

The translator desired to present a rendering of the poem that should attract the general reader. He regarded Simrock's version as too literal and archaic [1], the version of von Wolzogen as not sufficiently clear and beautiful [2], and the version of Heyne as not sufficiently varied in form [3] (Vorwort, i). He regards the *Beowulf* as of great importance in inspiring patriotism—he always calls the poem German—and even offers a comparison of *Beowulf* with Emperor William I. With the scholarship of his subject the author hardly seems concerned.

Text, and Relation of Parts.

The translation is founded on Grein's text of 1867 [4].

In addition to the translation, the volume contains articles on the history of the text, origin, the Germanic hero-tales, the episodes, the esthetic value of the poem. These are decidedly subordinate in interest to the translation.

Nature of the Translation.

The translation is in the so-called Nibelungen measures. Archaisms and unnatural compounds are avoided.

The Finnsburg fragment is inserted in the text at line 1068, p. 44 of the volume. The episode is furnished with a beginning and ending original with Hoffmann.

[1] See supra, p. 59.
[3] See supra, p. 63.
[2] See supra, p. 68.
[4] See supra, p. 56.

EXTRACT.

VIERTES ABENTEUER.

VON BEOWULF'S SCHWIMMFAHRT.

Da hub der Sohn der Ecglaf, Hunferd, zu reden an;
Er sass dem Herrn der Schildinge zu Füssen, und begann
Kampfworte zu entbieten. Dass her Beowulf kam,
Der kühne Meerdurchsegler, schuf seinem Herzen bitter'n Gram.

Dass unter dem Himmel habe ein andrer Recke mehr,   5
Denn er, des Ruhms auf Erden, war ihm zu tragen schwer:
'Bist *der* Beówulf Du, der einst sich in der weiten Flut
Mit Breca mass im Schwimmen? Zu hoch vermass sich da Dein Mut!

'Ihr spranget in die Wellen, vermessen wagtet ihr
Das Leben in die Tiefe, aus Ruhm- und Ehrbegier!   10
Die Fahrt, die schreckensvolle, nicht Freund noch Feind verleiden
Euch konnte. Also triebet im Sund dahin ihr Beiden!

'Als ihr mit Euren Armen des Meeres Breite decktet,
Die Meeresstrassen masset, die Hände rudernd recktet
Durch Brandungswirbel gleitend, vom Wintersturm getrieben   15
Hoch auf die Wellen schäumten; ihr mühtet Euch der Nächte sieben!

'So rangt ihr mit den Wogen! Da wurde Dir entrafft
Der Sieg von ihm, im Schwimmen, sein war die gröss're Kraft,
Ihn trug der Hochflut Wallen am Morgen an den Strand
Der Hadurämen, bald er von da die süsse Heimat wiederfand.   20

'Im Lande der Brondinge wie gerne man ihn sah!
Zu seiner schönen Feste kam er wieder da,
Wo er zu eigen hatte Mannen, Burg und Ringe,
Der Sohn Beanstan's hatte geleistet sein Erbot Dir allerdinge!'

Criticism of the Translation.

Hoffmann's translation is certainly not a contribution to
scholarship. It is a sufficient condemnation of the volume
to quote the words of the Vorwort:—

'Die Uebersetzungen von Grein, Holder und Möller sind mir nicht
zugänglich gewesen, auch wie es scheint, nicht sehr bekannt.'

It is not surprising that Hoffmann is unacquainted with the
translations of Holder and Möller, as these works have

never been made; but that a German translator should ignore the version of Grein is a revelation indeed.

Even though a translator may not care to embody in his work any new interpretations, it is nevertheless his duty to base his translation on the best text that he can find. But apparently Hoffmann had never heard of the Heyne editions of the text, nor of the Grein-Wülker *Bibliothek*. He bases his translation on Grein's text of 1867. He evidently considered it a sufficient recommendation of his work to associate with it the name of Grein, not troubling himself to discover what advance had been made upon the work of that scholar.

Examples of antiquated renderings may be brought forward :—

P. 1, line 1, Wie grosse Ruhmesthaten.

    2, line 1, So soll mit Gaben werben im Vaterhause schon.

    21, line 15 (see Extract), Vom Wintersturm getrieben Hoch auf die Wellen schäumten.

    84, line 3, Mothrytho.

Petty inaccuracies due to the nature of the translation also appear. An example of this is seen on page 3, at the opening of the first canto—

Ueber Burg und Mannen nun herrschte manches Jahr
Beówulf der Schilding. Wie hold dem König war
Sein Volk! in allen Landen seinen Ruhm man pries
Als lange schon sein Vater von dieser Erde Leben liess.

Literary Criticism.

The translation resembles the work of Lumsden[1] and Wackerbarth[2] in affording a version of the tale easily readable. And the same criticism may be passed on the work of Hoffmann that was passed on the two Englishmen.

[1] See p. 79.   [2] See p. 45.

The style and medium chosen are not well fitted to render the spirit of the poem. The *Nibelungenlied* is a poem of the late twelfth century. The *Beowulf* at latest belongs to the eighth. To choose for the translation of *Beowulf*, therefore, a medium surcharged with reminiscence of a time, place, and style quite different from those of the original is certainly an error. It may find an audience where another and more faithful rendering would fail; but it will never win the esteem of scholars. In his introduction Hoffmann calls attention to the lack of variety in blank verse, but surely it does not have the monotony inherent in a recurring rime and strophe.

Again, rime and strophe force upon the author the use of words and phrases needed to pad out the verse or stanza. Attention must also be called to the fact that the original seldom affords a natural pause at the exact point demanded by the use of a strophic form. See the close of the following stanzas in the Extract: I, III, IV, V. One effect of the forced pause is that there is confusion in the use of kennings, which often have to do duty as subject in one stanza and as object in another stanza.

Commonplace expressions, incident perhaps upon the use of the measure, are not unfrequent. Thus

translates

> Gesagt! gethan!
>
> ond þæt geæfndon swā (line 538).

Traces of this are also found in the extract; see beginning of last stanza.

In conclusion, it may be said that Hoffmann's version marks an advance in one way only, readableness; and in this it is hardly superior to Heyne's rendering, which has the advantage of scholarship.

MORRIS AND WYATT'S TRANSLATION

Colophon: Here endeth the story of Beowulf done out of the old English tongue by William Morris and A. J. Wyatt, and printed by said William Morris at the Kelmscott Press, Uppermall, Hammersmith, in the county of Middlesex, and finished on the tenth day of January, 1895. Large 4°, pp. vi, 119.

Troy type. Edition limited to 300 copies on paper and eight on vellum.

Second edition. The Tale of Beowulf, Sometime King of the Folk of the Weder Geats, translated by William Morris and A. J. Wyatt. London and New York: Longmans, Green, & Co., 1895. 8°, pp. x, 191.

Ninth English Translation. Imitative Measures.

Differences between the First and Second Editions.

In the second edition a title-page is added. The running commentary, printed in rubric on the margin of the first edition, is omitted.

Text Used.

The translation is, in general, conformed to Wyatt's text of 1894, departing from it in only a few unimportant details.

Part Taken in the Work by Morris and Wyatt respectively.

The matter is fortunately made perfectly clear in Mackail's *Life of William Morris*, vol. ii. p. 284 :—

'(Morris) was not an Anglo-Saxon scholar, and to help him in following the original, he used the aid of a prose translation made for him by Mr. A. J. Wyatt, of Christ's College, Cambridge, with whom he had also read through the original. The plan of their joint

labours had been settled in the autumn of 1892. Mr. Wyatt began
to supply Morris with his prose paraphrase in February, 1893, and
he at once began to "rhyme up," as he said, "very eager to be at
it, finding it the most delightful work." He was working at it all
through the year, and used to read it to Burne-Jones regularly on
Sunday mornings in summer.'

The plan of joining with his own the name of his principal
teacher was one which Morris had used before when translating from a foreign tongue. He published his rendering
of the *Volsunga Saga* as the work of ' Eirikr Magnússon
and William Morris.' There is no evidence that Mr. Wyatt
had any hand in forming the final draft of the translation.
In defending it, Morris took all the responsibility for the
book upon himself, and he always spoke of it as his own
work. In writing to a German student toward the end of
his life Morris spoke of the translation as his own without
mentioning Mr. Wyatt [1]. Nor has Mr. Wyatt shown a
disposition to claim a share in the work. In the preface
to his edition of the text of *Beowulf* (Cambridge, 1894), he
says:—

' Mr. William Morris has taken the text of this edition as the basis
of his modern metrical rendering of the lay.'—Page xiii.

Finally, it may be added that the specimens of Mr.
Wyatt's translation printed in the glossary and notes of
his book bear no resemblance to the work of Morris.

Morris's Theory of Translation.

None despised the merely literal rendering of an epic
poem more than William Morris. In writing of his version
of the *Odyssey* to Ellis, Morris said: ' My translation is
a real one so far, not a mere periphrase of the original as
all the others are.' In translating an ancient poem, he
tried to reproduce the simplicity and remoteness of phrase
which he found in his original. He believed it possible,

[1] See Mackail's *Life*, i. 198.

e. g., to suggest the archaic flavor of Homer by adopting a diction that bore the same relation to modern English that the language of Homer bore to that of the age of Pericles. The archaism of the English would represent the archaism of the Greek. This method he used in rendering Vergil and Homer.

But when he approached the translation of *Beowulf*, he was confronted by a new problem. It was evident that fifteenth-century English was ill-adapted to convey any just notion of eighth-century English. *Beowulf* required a diction older than that of Sir Thomas Malory or Chaucer. Hence it became necessary to discard the theory altogether, or else to produce another style which should in some true sense be imitative of *Beowulf*. This latter Morris tried to accomplish by increasing the archaism of his style by every means in his power. This feature is discussed in the following section.

Nature of the Translation.

The translation of *Beowulf* is written in extremely archaic language. An imitative measure of four principal stresses is used. Wherever possible, the Old English syntax has been preserved (see line 1242); the word-order of the original is retained. The archaic language is wrought of several different kinds of words. In the first place, there is the 'legitimate archaism,' such as 'mickle,' 'burg,' 'bairn'; there are forms which are more closely associated with the translation of Old English, such as 'middle-garth,' 'ring-stem.' There are modern words used with the old signification, such as 'kindly' (in the sense 'of the same kind'), 'won war' (in the sense 'wage war'), 'fret' (in the sense 'eat'). Finally, there are forms which are literally translated from Old English: 'the sight seen once only' from *ansȳn*, face, 251 ; 'spearman' from *garsecg*, ocean (see extract), 'gift-scat' from *gif-sceatt*, gift of money,

378; 'the Maker's own making' from *metod-sceaft*, doom,
1180. Romance words are excluded whenever possible.
A glossary of 'some words not commonly used now' is
included in the book, but none of the words cited above,
save 'burg,' is found in it.

EXTRACT.

IX. UNFERTH CONTENDETH IN WORDS WITH BEOWULF.

Spake out then Unferth that bairn was of Ecglaf,
And he sat at the feet of the lord of the Scyldings,   500
He unbound the battle-rune; was Beowulf's faring,
Of him the proud mere-farer, mickle unliking,
Whereas he begrudg'd it of any man other
That he glories more mighty the middle-garth over
Should hold under heaven than he himself held:
Art thou that Beowulf who won strife with Breca
On the wide sea contending in swimming,
When ye two for pride's sake search'd out the floods
And for a dolt's cry into deep water
Thrust both your life-days? No man the twain of you,   510
Lief or loth were he, might lay wyte to stay you
Your sorrowful journey, when on the sea row'd ye;
Then when the ocean-stream ye with your arms deck'd,
Meted the mere-streets, there your hands brandish'd!
O'er the Spearman ye glided; the sea with waves welter'd,
The surge of the winter. Ye twain in the waves' might
For a seven nights swink'd. He outdid thee in swimming,
And the more was his might; but him in the morn-tide
To the Heatho-Remes' land the holm bore ashore,
And thence away sought he to his dear land and lovely,   520
The lief to his people sought the land of the Brondings,
The fair burg peace-warding, where he the folk owned,
The burg and the gold rings. What to theeward he boasted,
Beanstan's son, for thee soothly he brought it about.

Criticism of the Translation.

The Morris-Wyatt translation is thoroughly accurate,
and is, so to speak, an official commentary on the text

of Wyatt's edition. It is therefore of importance to the student of the *Beowulf*.

As a literary rendering the translation is disappointing. In the first place, it must be frankly avowed that the diction is frequently so strange that it seems to modern readers well-nigh ridiculous. There are certain sentences which cannot but evoke a smile. Such are: ' (he) spoke a word backward,' line 315; 'them that in Scaney dealt out the scat,' line 1686.

Secondly, the translation is unreadable. There is an avalanche of archaisms. One example of the extreme obscurity may be given :—

'Then rathe was beroom'd, as the rich one was bidding,
For the guests a-foot going the floor all withinward.'

l. 1975-76.

It would seem that the burden of 'rathe,' 'beroomed,' and 'withinward,' were sufficient for any sentence to carry, but we are left to discover for ourselves that 'rich one' does not mean rich one, but ruler, that the 'floor' is not a floor but a hall, and that the guests are not guests, but the ruler's own men.

Morris himself was conscious of the obscurity of the work :—

'For the language of his version Morris once felt it necessary to make an apology. Except a few words, he said, the words used in it were such as he would not hesitate to use in an original poem of his own. He did not add, however, that their effect, if slipped sparingly in amid his own pellucid construction and facile narrative method, would be very different from their habitual use in a translation . . . As the work advanced, he seems to have felt this himself, and his pleasure in the doing of it fell off.'—Mackail's *Life*, ii. 284-5.

Finally, the version does not *translate*. Words like 'Spearman' for *Ocean*, and combinations like 'the sight seen once only' for *the face*, can be understood only by the intimate student of Old English poetry, and there is no reason why such a person should not peruse *Beowulf* in the original tongue rather than in a translation occasionally as obscure as the poem itself.

If one can peer through the darkness of Morris's diction, he will discover a fairly pleasing use of the so-called imitative measure. The verse is not nearly so rough as the original; many of the characteristic substitutions are avoided. There is evident a tendency toward the 'rising verse' and the anapestic foot. The feminine ending is frequently used. The verse is, therefore, not strictly imitative in that it retains the Old English system of versification, but rather in that it attempts to suggest the Old English movement by the use of four principal stresses and a varying number of unstressed syllables. Morris's verse is the best of all the 'imitative' measures.

SIMONS'S TRANSLATION

Beówulf, Angelsaksisch Volksepos, vertaald in Stafrijm, en met Inleiding en Aanteekeningen voorzien door Dr. L. Simons, Briefwisselend Lid der Koninklijke Vlaamsche Academie voor Taal- en Letterkunde, Leeraar aan 't koninklijk Athenaeum te Brussel. Gent, A. Siffer, 1896. Large 8°, pp. 355.

Published for the Koninklijke Vlaamsche Academie voor Taal- en Letterkunde.

First Dutch Translation. Iambic Pentameter.

Aim and Contents of the Volume.

The author's purpose, as stated in 'Een Woord Vooraf,' is to make the *Beowulf* better known to the Dutch public. With this in view he adds to his translation copious notes and an exhaustive comment. The titles of his various chapters are: De Beschaving in den Beowulf, Christendom,

Heldensage en Volksepos, Geschiedenis, Mythos, Geatas, Nationaliteit van den Beowulf, Tijd van Voltooiing, Het Handschrift, De Versbouw, Epische Stijl, Innerlijke Geschiednis. Explanatory and critical comment is given in the footnotes, and textual criticism in the Notes at the end of the volume.

Text Used.

'I have followed the text of Socin[1]; where I have preferred to give another reading I have justified my proceeding in the Notes at the end of the work.'—Een Woord Vooraf.

Nature of the Translation.

It is a literal translation in iambic pentameter.

'Of the translation nothing in particular needs to be said. I have followed my original as closely as possible.'—Een Woord Vooraf.

He adds that this was no easy task, as Dutch does not afford the same variety of simile as the Old English.

A page is then given to the discussion of the nature of his verse. He first gives his reasons for preferring iambic pentameter to the 'Reinartsvers,' which some might think best to use.

'Moreover, the iambic pentameter lends itself well to division into hemistichs, the principal characteristic of the ancient epic versification.'—Een Woord Vooraf.

He has often preferred the simple alliteration (aa, bb) to the Old English system[2].

EXTRACT.

IX.

En Hunferd zeide toen, de zoon van Ecglaf,
    Die aan die voeten zat des Schyldingvorsten,
    Het kampgeheim ontkeetnend : (Beowulfs aankomst,

---

[1] Fifth edition of Heyne's text, 1888.
[2] At this point Simons speaks as if ab, ab, were the common form of alliteration in Old English, whereas it is rather uncommon.

Des koenen golfvaart gaf hem grooten aanstoot,
Omdat hij geenszins aan een ander gunde
Der mannen, meerder roem op aard te rapen,
Beneên de wolken, dan hem was geworden.)
'Zijt gij die Beowulf, die met Brecca aanbond
Den wedstrijd op de wijde zee, in 't zwemmen
Met dezen streven dorst, toen boud gij beiden
Navorschtet in den vloed en gij uit grootspraak
Uw leven waagdet in het diepe water?
Geen stervling was in staat, noch vriend noch vijand,
De roekelooze reis u af te raden.
Toen braakt gij beiden roeiend door de baren
En dektet onder uwen arm de deining,
Gij maat de zeebahn, zwaaiend met de handen,
Doorgleedt de waterwieling, schoon met golven
De kil opklotste bij des winters branding.
Op deze wijze wurmdet gij te gader
Wel zeven nachten in 't bezit der zeeën.
Doch gene ging in vaart u ver te boven ;
Hij had toch meerder macht. De strooming stuwde
Hem met den morgen heen ten Headoraemen,
Van waar hij wedervond, de volksgevierde,
Het lieve stambezit, het land der Brondings,
De schoone schatburg, waar hij wapenlieden
En goed en goud bezat. De zoon van Beanstan
Hield tegen u geheel zijn woord in waarheid.'

Criticism of the Translation.

The translation seems to aim chiefly at accuracy, which accounts for the rather large number of notes containing readings suggested by various commentators. The translator uses freely compounds and metaphors similar to those in the original text. This seems occasionally to militate against the clearness of the work. Thus, it is doubtful whether 'kampgeheim ontkeetnend' of the extract conveys to the modern Dutch reader any notion similar to that of the Old English *beadu-runen onband*.

The present writer is unable to offer any literary criticism of the translation.

STEINECK'S TRANSLATION

Altenglische Dichtungen (Beowulf, Elene, u. a.) in wortgetreuer Uebersetzung von H. Steineck. Leipzig, 1898, O. R. Reisland. 8°, Beowulf, pp. 1–102. Seventh German Translation. Line for line.

Aim of the Volume, and Nature of the Translation.

'Die vorliegende Uebersetzung ist aus dem Bedürfnis einer wortgetreuen Wiedergabe altenglischer Denkmäler entstanden. Soweit es der Sinn zuliess, ist das Bestreben dahin gegangen, für jedes altenglische Wort das etymologisch entsprechende neuhochdeutsche, wenn vorhanden, einzusetzen. So ist die Uebersetzung zugleich ein sprachgeschichtliches Werk.'—Vorwort.

Text Used.

The translation is based on Heyne's text of 1863 [1] (Vorwort). Fragmentary passages are not restored.

EXTRACT.

IX.

500 Hunferd sprach, des Ecgláf Sohn,
    Welcher zu Füssen sass des Herren der Scyldinge;
    Er löste der Streiter Geheimniss—ihm war Beowulfs Fahrt,
    Des mutigen Meerfahrers, zu grossem Neid,
    Weil er nicht gönnte, dass irgend ein anderer
    Jemals nun mehr Ruhmesthaten
    Unter dem Himmel der Erde erwarb als er selbst:
    'Bist du Bêowulf, der du mit Breca kämpftest
    Auf weiter See in einem Wettschwimmen,
    Dort durchforschtet ihr beide aus Stolz die Fluten
    Und wagtet aus verwegener Ruhmsucht im tiefen Wasser
510 Euer Leben? Euch beiden konnte keiner,
    Weder Freund noch Feind, vorwerfen

[1] See supra, p. 64.

Die gefahrvolle Reise; da rudertet ihr beide im Wasser,
Dort überdecktet ihr beide den Wasserstrom mit Armen,
Ihr masst die Meeresstrassen, mit Händen schwangt ihr,
Ihr glittet über die Flut; das Meer wallte in Fluten,
Des Winters Gewoge; ihr mühtet euch in des Wassers Gewalt
Sieben Nächte ab; er besiegte dich beim Schwimmen,
Er hatte grössere Kraft. Da warf ihn in der Morgenzeit
An das Headoræmenland die See,
520 Von dort aus suchte er das traute Stammgut auf,
Der seinen Leuten Teure, das Land der Brondinge,
Die schöne Friedensburg, wo er Volk besass,
Burg und Ringe. Alles, wozu er sich dir verpflichtete,
Leistete der Sohn Bêanstâns wahrhaftig.'

Criticism of the Translation.

It would be manifestly unfair to criticize this translation
for its want of grace and melody, because it is avowedly
a literal rendering, and a literal rendering makes no attempt
to attain these qualities. But there are certain things
which are indispensable in a good literal translation. It
is imperative that such a translation should be based on
the best text of the original poem. What has Steineck
done? He has gone back thirty-five years and chosen an
early and inaccurate edition of a work that has been five
times re-edited, Heyne's text of 1863! It seems almost
incredible that a German, living in the midst of scholars
who have done more than any other people to interpret
the *Beowulf*, should ignore the fruits of their efforts.

It is unnecessary to enumerate the faults of this translation due to dependence upon an antiquated edition of
the text. Suffice it to say that when the edition of 1863
was printed the text had not yet been properly transcribed
from the MS.[1]

But there are evidences of an inaccuracy of a different
kind that betray a carelessness utterly reprehensible. The

---

[1] See also supra, p. 8.

H

author is apparently unable to transliterate properly the Old English names. Thus he has Vealhpeon and Vealhpeo (for Wealhtheow), Ecgpeow, Halbdaene (for Healfdene), Ermanarich, &c.

In his attempt to produce an etymological document, the translator uses many compounds such as even the German language might be better without; such are—Sippenschar (sibbegedriht), 730; Schattenwandler (sceadugenga), 704; Wangenpolster (hlēor-bolster), 689; Leibpanzer (līc-syrce), 550. As compounds these may not be offensive to a German; but the trouble with them is that they do not translate the Old English ideas.

Finally, it may be asked why a translation that appeals only as a literal rendering should not be strictly literal, noting its every variation from the original, italicizing supplied words, holding to the original word-order.

Steineck's translation did not advance the interpretation of *Beowulf* a whit. In point of accuracy the book is not worthy to stand with good translations thirty years old.

J. R. C. HALL'S TRANSLATION

Beowulf, and the Fight at Finnsburg, a translation into modern English prose, with an Introduction and Notes, by John R. Clark Hall, M.A., Ph.D. With twelve illustrations[1]. London : Swan Sonnenschein and Company, Lim., 1901. 8°, pp. xlv, 203.

Tenth English Translation. Prose.

[1] Chiefly of Anglo-Saxon antiquities.

Translator, and Circumstances of Publication.

Hitherto Dr. Hall had been chiefly known to the learned world for his excellent *Anglo-Saxon Dictionary for Students.*

Up to this time no prose translation had appeared in England since 1876, save Earle's[1], which for the elementary student was practically useless. Moreover, this translation was the first to embody the results of various studies on the poem during the past decade.

Contents.

Unlike the preceding works on *Beowulf*, it may be said that the introductory and illustrative matter in this book is of quite as much importance as the translation. The author says of his book :—

' The following pages comprise a short statement of what is actually known with respect to the poem of *Beowulf*, another statement of what seems to me most likely to be true amongst the almost innumerable matters of conjecture concerning it, and a few words of literary appreciation.'—Introduction, p. ix.

Statements similar to these have been put forth by other translators of the poem, but the material of their volume has not always borne them out. The studies of the poem in the Introduction are sufficient for a school edition of *Beowulf*—a similar body of information is not found in any of the existing editions—while annotations of some importance to the elementary student are found in the notes and running comment. The book contains, beside the translation, a discussion of the form, language, geographical allusions, date, and composition of the poem, as well as a useful, though inaccurate, bibliography[2].

[1] See supra, p. 91.
[2] See my forthcoming review of the book in the *Journal of Germanic Philology.*

Text Used.

The translation is founded on the text of A. J. Wyatt, Cambridge, 1894. Dr. Hall does not always follow the interpretations given in Wyatt's glossary, nor is the punctuation of the translation conformed to that of the Old English text.

Indebtedness to Preceding Scholars.

In his translation Dr. Hall seems to be most indebted to the work of Professor Earle [1] (see lines 4, 71, 517, 852, 870, 926, 996, 1213, 1507, 2021, 3034, &c.).

Frequent reference is also made to the work of Cosijn, *Aanteekeningen op den Beowulf* (1892). The work of other scholars, such as Bugge, Heyne, Socin, is also referred to.

Nature of the Translation.

The translation is a literal prose version. It is constantly interrupted by bits of running comment, designed to overcome the inherent obscurity of the poem, or to afford an elaborate digest of the story if read without the translation (p. 7 .

The rendering avoids archaisms.

Bugge's restoration is used at line 3150 ; the passage at line 2215 is not restored.

EXTRACT.
VIII.

UNFERTH TAUNTS BEOWULF. BEOWULF'S CONTEST WITH BRECA.
(Lines 499-558.)

(499–505). *Now comes a jarring note. Unferth, a Danish courtier, is devoured by jealousy, and taunts Beowulf.*

Then Unferth, the son of Ecglaf, who sat at the feet of the lord of the Scyldings, spoke, and gave vent to secret thoughts of strife,—the

[1] See supra, p. 91.

journey of Beowulf, the brave sea-farer, was a great chagrin to him, for he grudged that any other man under heaven should ever obtain more glory on this middle-earth than he himself.

(506–528). '*Art thou the same Beowulf,*' says he, '*who ventured on a foolhardy swimming match with Breca on the open sea in winter, for seven days, and got beaten ? A worse fate is in store for thee when thou meetest Grendel !*'

' Art thou that Beowulf who strove with Breca, contested with him on the open sea, in a swimming contest, when ye two for vainglory tried the floods, and ventured your lives in deep water for idle boasting ? Nor could any man, friend or foe, dissuade you from your sorry enterprise when ye swam on the sea ; when ye compassed the flowing stream with your arms, meted out the sea-paths, battled with your hands, and glided over the ocean ; when the sea, the winter's flood, surged with waves. Ye two toiled in the water's realm seven nights ; he overcame you at swimming, he had the greater strength. Then, at morning time, the ocean cast him up on the Heathoræmas' land. Thence, dear to his people, he sought his beloved fatherland, the land of the Brondings, his fair stronghold-city, where he had subjects and treasures and a borough. The son of Beanstan performed faithfully all that he had pledged himself to. So I expect for thee a worse fatality,—though thou hast everywhere prevailed in rush of battle,— gruesome war,—if thou darest await Grendel at close quarters for the space of a night.'

Criticism of the Translation.

The extract is typical of all that is best in the translation. It is a thoroughly accurate piece of work, failing only where Wyatt's edition of the text is unsatisfactory. Translations like ' gave vent to secret thoughts of strife ' and ' thou hast prevailed in the rush of battle ' show that the work is the outcome of long thought and deep appreciation. At times the translation, as here, verges on a literary rendering. But in this respect the first part of the poem is vastly superior to the later parts, though all three are marred by extreme literalness. Dr. Hall did not always escape the strange diction that has so often before disfigured the translations of *Beowulf* :—

Line 2507, 'my unfriendly hug finished his bony frame.'
  „   2583, 'The Geat's free-handed friend crowed not in
            pride of victory.'
  „   2655, 'Fell the foe and shield the Weder-Geat
            Lord's life.
  „   2688, 'the public scourge, the dreadful salamander.'
  „   2834, 'show his form' (said of the Dragon).
  „   2885, 'hopelessly escheated from your breed.'

It is also rather surprising to learn from Dr. Hall that
Beowulf was one of those that 'advanced home government' (l. 3005).

It should be added that the explanatory comment which
constantly interrupts the translation, often six or eight
times in a section, is annoying, both because it distracts
the attention and because it is often presented in a style
wholly inappropriate to the context.

But this absence of ease and dignity does not hinder
Dr. Hall's translation from being an excellent rendering
of the matter of the poem, at once less fanciful than
Earle's [1] and more modern than Garnett's [2], its only rivals
as a literal translation.   That it conveys an adequate
notion of the style of *Beowulf*, however, it is impossible
to affirm.

TINKER'S TRANSLATION

Beowulf, translated out of the Old English by Chauncey
Brewster Tinker, M.A.   New York: Newson and Co., 1902.
12°, pp. 158.

Eleventh English Translation.   Prose.

[1] See supra, p. 91.   [2] See supra, p. 83.

Aim of the Volume and Nature of the Translation.

'The present translation of *Beowulf* is an attempt to make as simple and readable a version of the poem as is consistent with the character of the original. Archaic forms, which have been much in favor with translators of Old English, have been excluded, because it has been thought that vigor and variety are not incompatible with simple, idiomatic English. . . .

The principal ways in which the present version differs from a merely literal translation are the following: (1) in a rather broad interpretation of pregnant words and phrases ; (2) in a conception of some of the Old English compounds as conventional phrases in which the original metaphorical sense is dead ; (3) in a free treatment of connecting words ; (4) in frequent substitution of a proper name for an ambiguous pronoun.

The translation is based on the text of A. J. Wyatt (Cambridge, 1898) ; a few departures from his readings are enumerated in the Notes.'—Preface, pp. 5, 6.

EXTRACT.

VIII AND IX.

Unferth, a thane of Hrothgar, grows jealous of Beowulf and taunts him, raking up old tales of a swimming-match with Breca. Beowulf is angered and boastfully tells the truth touching that adventure, and puts Unferth to silence. Queen Wealhtheow passes the cup. Hrothgar commends Heorot to the care of Beowulf.

UNFERTH, the son of Ecglaf, who sat at the feet of the lord of the Scyldings, spoke, and stirred up a quarrel; the coming of Beowulf, the brave seafarer, vexed him sore, for he would not that any other man under heaven should ever win more glories in this world than he himself. 'Art thou that Beowulf who didst strive with Breca on the broad sea and didst contend with him in swimming, when ye two, foolhardy, made trial of the waves and for a mad boast risked your lives in the deep water ? None, friend or foe, could turn you from the sorry venture when ye two swam out upon the sea. But ye enfolded the ocean-streams with your arms, measured the sea-streets, buffeted the water with your hands, gliding over the deep. The ocean was tossing with waves, a winter's sea. Seven nights ye toiled in the power of the waters ; and he overcame thee in the match, for he had the greater strength. Then at morning-tide the sea cast him up on the coast of the Heathoræmas, whence he, beloved of his people, went to his dear fatherland, the country of the Brondings, and his own fair city where he was lord of a stronghold, and of subjects and treasure. Verily, the son of Beanstan made good all his boast against thee. Wherefore, though thou hast ever been valiant in the rush of battle, I look to a grim fight, yea, and a worse issue, for thee, if thou darest for the space of one night abide near Grendel.'

APPENDIX I

INCOMPLETE TRANSLATIONS, AND PARAPHRASES

LEO'S DIGEST

Bëówulf, dasz[1] älteste deutsche in angelsächsischer mundart erhaltene heldengedicht nach seinem inhalte, und nach seinen historischen und mythologischen beziehungen betrachtet. Ein beitrag zur geschichte alter deutscher geisteszustände. Von H. Leo. Halle, bei Eduard Anton, 1839. 8°, pp. xx, 120.

Selections Translated into German Prose.

Contents of the Volume, and Nature of the Translation.
This was the first German book to give any extended account of the poem. The titles of the chapters are : I. Historische Anlehnung ; II. Mythischer Inhalt ; III. Die geographischen Angaben; IV. Genealogische Verhältnisse der in dem Liede vorkommenden Helden ; V. Uebersicht des Inhalts des Gedichtes von Bëówulf. In this fifth chapter are found the extracts from *Beowulf.* It will be seen that the chapter is somewhat subordinate to the others, its chief purpose being to furnish a kind of digest of the poem, to be used principally as a work of reference. A desire to condense leads the translator to omit lines that he does not deem essential to

---

[1] Leo was a spelling reformer.

an understanding of the events and characters of the poem. Unfortunately his omissions are often the most poetical lines of the *Beowulf.* For example, he omits the description of Beowulf's sea-voyage; Hrothgar's account of the haunt of Grendel and his dam is curtailed; the dying words of Beowulf, perhaps the most beautiful lines in the poem, are clipped. Further examples may be found in the extract given below. This insufficiency is excused by the fact that Leo's main object in preparing the book was to prove certain theories that he held respecting the origin and date of the poem. The text from which he translates is Kemble's [1].

EXTRACT.

ACHTER GESANG.

Hûnferđ Ecglâfs sohn, der zu des scildingenfürsten füssen sasz, began da ein streiterregendesz gespräch; denn er wird eifersüchtig auf den rum, den Bëówulf sich zu erwerben geht. Er selbst wil der berümteste sein unter den wolken. Er sagte: 'Bistu der Bëówulf, der mit Brëcca ein wetschwimmen hielt sieben tage und nächte lang, bis er dich in schwimmen besigte, der kräftigere man; dann am achten morgen stig er auf Heáđorämes ansz land und gieng heim zu den Brondingen, wo er eine burg und edlesz gefolge und reichtum hatte? Bëánstânes sohn hat dir allesz geleistet, wasz er gewettet hatte.'

Omissions :—
Line 502, mōdges mere-faran.
  „   507–517 *entire.*
  „   520, swǣsne ēđel, lēof his lēodum.

Criticism of the Extract.

As an analysis this is good enough; as a translation of the passage it is of course utterly inadequate—it omits the very best lines in the original. The book served, however, as a running digest of the story, and as such gave an

[1] See supra, p. 33.

excellent idea of the contents of the poem. But Ettmüller was justified in calling the translation which he published the next year, 'the first German translation[1].'

SANDRAS'S ACCOUNT

De carminibus anglo-saxonicis Cædmoni adjudicatis Disquisitio. Has theses Parisiensi Litterarum Facultati proponebat S. G. Sandras in Lycaeo Claromontensi Professor. Parisiis, Apud A. Durand, Bibliopolam, 1859. 8°, pp. 87. Beowulf described *Cap. Primum*, § 2, De Profana Poesi, pp. 10-19.

Extracts Translated into Latin Prose.

The only significance of this book is that it contained the first information about *Beowulf* given to the French public. About ten lines are literally translated in Cap. I, § 1, all under the general title, De Poesi Saxonica. In § 2 the poem is rather carefully sketched, much after the manner of Leo[2], from Beowulf's arrival in the Danish land to the fight with Grendel.

E. H. JONES'S PARAPHRASE

Popular Romances of the Middle Ages. By George W. Cox, M.A., and Eustace Hinton Jones. London: Longmans, Green, & Co., 1871. 8°, *Beowulf* (by E. H. Jones), pp. 382-398.

*Second edition, in one volume (containing, in addition to the romances in the first edition, those formerly published

---

[1] See supra, p. 37.   [2] See supra, p. 122.

under the title 'Tales of the Teutonic Lands'). C. Kegan
Paul & Company: London, 1880 (1879).

A Paraphrase for General Readers.

Aim of the Volume.

'The thought that these old romances may be presented to Englishmen of the present day in a form which shall retain their real vigour without the repulsive characteristics impressed on them by a comparatively rude and ignorant age may not, perhaps, be regarded as inexcusably presumptuous. With greater confidence it may be affirmed that, if we turn to these old legends or romances at all, it should be for the purpose of learning what they really were, and not with any wish of seeing them through a glass which shall reflect chiefly our own thoughts about them and throw over them a colouring borrowed from the sentiment of the nineteenth century.

'These two conditions have, it is hoped, been strictly observed in the versions here given of some of the great romances of mediæval Europe. While special care has been taken to guard against the introduction even of phrases not in harmony with the original narratives, not less pains have been bestowed on the task of preserving all that is essential in the narrative ; and thus it may perhaps be safely said that the readers of this volume will obtain from it an adequate knowledge of these time-honoured stories, without having their attention and their patience overtaxed by a multiplicity of superfluous and therefore utterly irksome details.'—Preface, pp. vi, vii.

Nature of the Paraphrase.

The poem is relieved of all the episodes except the prolog and King Hrothgar's discourse. Sometimes these omissions seem unnecessary. It is certainly a mistake to sacrifice the swimming-match, lively in its narrative, dramatic in setting.

On the other hand, the author makes an attempt to preserve as much as possible of the original style. So anxious is he to save every picturesque word of the original, that he sometimes transfers expressions from the passages which he is obliged to drop and inserts them in other parts of the story.

Extract [1].

' Away to the westward among the people of the Geáts lived a man, strongest of his race, tall, mighty-handed, and clean made. He was a thane, kinsman to Hygelác the Geátish chief, and nobly born, being son of Ecgtheow the Wægmunding, a war-prince who wedded with the daughter of Hrethel the Geát. This man heard of Grendel's deeds, of Hrothgár's sorrow, and the sore distress of the Danes, and having sought out fifteen warriors, he entered into a new-pitched ship to seek the war-king across the sea. Bird-like the vessel's swan-necked prow breasted the white sea-foam till the warriors reached the windy walls of cliff and the steep mountains of the Danish shores. They thanked God because the wave-ways had been easy to them ; then, sea-wearied, lashed their wide-bosomed ship to an anchorage, donned their war-weeds, and came to Heorot, the gold and jewelled house. Brightly gleamed their armour and merrily sang the ring-iron of their trappings as they marched into the palace.'—Pages 384–5.

Criticism of the Paraphrase.

The object of a paraphrase is to present all the essential matter of the original, in a style materially simpler than, though not unrelated to, the original.

The matter of Mr. Jones's paraphrase is not above criticism. It is full of minor errors. In the extract, for example, the original does not say that the heroes ' donned their war-weeds,' nor that there were mountains on the shores of Denmark.

The style of the work is much better. It is throughout strong and clear, not over-sentimental. It is, perhaps, too intimate ; it savors slightly of the *Märchen*. This absence of vigor and remoteness may be due to the nature of the volume of which this paraphrase is only a part.

[1] Swimming-match omitted.

ZINSSER'S SELECTION

Jahresbericht über die Realschule zu Forbach (Lothringen) für das Schuljahr 1880 bis 1881, mit welchem zu der öffentlichen Prüfung am Freitag den 12. August 1881 ergebenst einladet der Director A. Knitterscheid. Voran geht eine Abhandlung des ordentlichen Lehrers G. Zinsser: Der 'Kampf Beowulfs mit Grendel,' als Probe einer metrischen Uebersetzung des angelsächsischen Epos 'Beóvulf.' Saarbrücken. Druck von Gebrüder Hofer. 1881. 4°, pp. 18, double columns, Schulnachrichten 6. The First 836 Lines translated in Iambic Pentameter.

Aim, Contents, and Method of Translation.

'Gleichwol wird das Gedicht in deutscher Sprache noch wenig gelesen ; und es mag darum gerechtfertigt sein, wenn auch ein weniger Berufener ein Schärflein zum weiteren Bekanntwerden dieses altehrwürdigen Erzeugnisses germanischen Geistes beitragen will. Derselbe hat in seiner Uebersetzung, von welcher im Folgenden von 3184 Versen nur die ersten 826 [1], nämlich der Kampf Beowulfs mit Grendel mit vorausgehender Genealogie der dänischen Könige, vorgeführt werden, alles vermieden, was dem Laien das Verständnis erschweren könnte. Die am Schluss beigefügten mythologischen, historischen und geographischen Erläuterungen können auch denen willkommen sein, welche sich eingehender mit dem Gedicht beschäftigen wollen.'— Einleitung, 4.

Text Used.

The text used is Heyne's edition of 1873 (see Einleitung, 4).

EXTRACT.

9.

Doch Hunferd, Ecglafs Sohn, der beim Gelage
Zu Füssen Hrodgars, seines Herren, sass,
War voll Verdruss, der Ruhm des Beowulf
Erregte bittren Neid im Busen ihm.

[1] According to the Old English text, 836.

Er konnte nicht ertragen, wenn beim Volke
Ein andrer mehr gepriesen ward, als er.
Voll Aerger sucht' er Händel, also sprechend:
' Du bist gewiss der Beowulf, der einst
Im Meer mit Breca um die Wette schwamm?
Ihr masset damals euch in kühnem Wagen!
Das mühevolle Werk euch auszureden
Vermochte niemand, tollkühn setztet ihr
Das Leben ein und schwammt ins Meer hinaus.
Zerteiltet mit den Armen kraftgemut
Des Meeres Wogen, glittet rasch dahin
In kalter Flut. Ihr mühtet sieben Nächte
Euch ab, und endlich siegte Brecas Stärke,
Er war dir doch voran an Heldenkraft.
Ihn trug die Flut zur Morgenzeit hinauf
Zum Hadorämenstrand. Von dort gelangt'
Er dann zu seiner Burg in Brondingland,
Die, starkbefestigt, funkelndes Geschmied,
Der Spangen und Juwelen viele birgt.
Es jubelte sein Volk dem Herren zu,
Der kühn sein Wort gelöst, nachdem er so
Im Wettkampf glänzend hatte obgesiegt!'

Criticism of the Extract.

The translation is very free. Lines that are obscure in the original are not allowed to be obscure in the translation, even if they have to have a meaning read into them. For example, in the extract quoted above, *beadu-runen onband* of the original is rendered 'sucht' er Händel,' thoroughly intelligible, but not accurate. There is at times a tendency to paraphrase, or even to introduce an original sentence into the poem. An example of this may be seen at the close of the first canto :—

' unerforschlich sind
Und dunkel oft die Wege des Geschickes[1].'—Page 5, I. 54.

[1] The Old English reads :—
Men ne cunnon
secgan tō sōðe, sele-rǽdende
hæleð under heofenum, hwā þǣm hlæste onfēng.—Lines 50–52.

Words are occasionally omitted. In the extract above *ne lēof nē lāđ* (l. 511) and *sunu Bēanstānes* (l. 524) are omitted in translation. There are no lines in the original which correspond to the last line and a half of the extract.

Of course by adopting this method of translation the writer attains his purpose. His poem is readable, but readable at the expense of accuracy. As a paraphrase, the version is commendable; but it is hardly of importance in any other way.

GIBB'S PARAPHRASE

*Gudrun and other Stories, from the Epics of the Middle Ages, by John Gibb. M. Japp & Company: London: Edinburgh (printed), 1881.

Gudrun, Beowulf, and Roland, with other mediaeval tales by John Gibb, with twenty illustrations. Second edition. London: T. Fisher Unwin, 1884 (1883).

8°, *Beowulf*, pp. 135–168, with three illustrations [1].

A Paraphrase in English Prose.

Aim of the Volume.

'I have not translated them (the poems) literally, but have told their stories faithfully in simple language, with the special design of interesting young people, although I am not without hope that they will be read by some who can no longer be called young.'—Prefatory Note.

Nature of the Paraphrase.

The following parts are omitted: (1) All episodes except the Prolog; (2) All lines that do not have to do directly

---

[1] Woodcuts; two of them are identical with the ones given in the Wägner-MacDowall paraphrase: see infra, p. 130.

with the story; (3) All the descriptive adjectives and kennings of the poem.

Gibb seems to care nothing for the beauties of the style. How much he has sacrificed may be seen by noting his rendering of the celebrated description of Grendel's haunt :—

'I know not their home. It is in a dark lake overshadowed by trees. Into that lake the stag will not plunge, even although the hounds are close upon it, so fearful and unholy is the place.'

An illustration of the same thing may be seen by noting the omission of phrases from the swimming-match.

EXTRACT.

But Hunferth, the son of Ecglaf, who sat at the feet of King Hrothgar, was displeased. He was grieved that any hero should come to the land boasting that he could do what no one among the Danes could do. He said scornfully to Beowulf—

'Tell me, art thou the Beowulf whom Breca overcame in a swimming match ? I heard the tale. You both ventured out like foolish men among the waves in the days of winter. For seven nights you swam together, but Breca was the stronger. Thou wilt have a worse defeat shouldst thou venture to meet Grendel in the darkness of the night.'— Page 144.

Criticism of the Paraphrase.

In comparison with the work of Mr. Jones[1], it may be said that Mr. Gibb's paraphrase is fuller, reproduces more events, and follows more faithfully the original order. He supplies fewer explanatory words and sentences. But, on the other hand, Mr. Gibb's work, unlike Mr. Jones's, has no merits of style—it is all on a dead level of prose. Thus it sins against one of the laws of paraphrase : that the writer, in relieving himself of the exacting duties of translator, must present the story in a more literary and more truly adequate medium. Mr. Gibb's is one of the poorer paraphrases.

[1] See supra, p. 123.

I

Indebtedness to Arnold.

At page 280 of the concluding chapter, the author speaks of the history and character of the poem. It will be found on reference to this section that the author is a follower of the views set forth in the edition of Mr. Thomas Arnold[1]. It is probable that Mr. Gibb was indebted to this book for much of his paraphrase, but the free character of the version prevents any decision on this point.

THE WÄGNER-MACDOWALL PARAPHRASE

Epics and Romances of the Middle Ages. Adapted from the Work of Dr. W. Wägner by W. M. MacDowall, and edited by W. S. W. Anson. Philadelphia: J. B. Lippincott & Co., London: W. Swan Sonnenschein & Co., 1883. 8°, *Beowulf*, pp. 347–364, with two illustrations[2].
Second Edition, Oct. 1883.
Sixth Edition, 1890.
Eighth Edition, 1896.

Beowulf Retold, with Changes and Additions.

The paraphrase is adapted from *Deutsche Heldensagen für Schule und Haus*, by Dr. W. Wägner (Leipzig, 1881).

Aim of the Book.

From the nature of the changes made in the story, it is evident that an appeal is made to younger readers. This is borne out by the statement on p. 9 of the Introduction.

[1] See supra, p. 71.   [2] Woodcuts; inaccurate.

Changes in the Story.

The story does not pretend to do more than follow the most general outlines of the original. The most important changes are in the first division of the poem, where it would seem that no changes whatever were needed. The principal additions are the following :—

(1) A minstrel flees from plague-stricken Heorot, sails to the Geatish land, and sings the terror wrought by Grendel, urging Beowulf to come and save the people.

(2) The swimming-match is introduced into the action of the story, with the *motif* radically altered. Breca is represented as winning the match.

(3) The incident of Beowulf's refusal of the crown is amplified and introduced into the story at the opening of the third part.

(4) The story differs from the original in a number of minor details.

EXTRACT.

The minstrel tuned his harp and sang of Beowulf's heroic deeds, and prophesied that he would conquer and slay the monster of the morass. This praise made Hunford, one of the courtiers, angry and jealous. He said it was Breka, not Beowulf, that had won the golden chain [1]; that the Gothic hero was undertaking an enterprise that would very likely lead him to his death; and he advised him to think twice before attacking Grendel. Upon this, Beowulf exclaimed indignantly that he had won a good sword instead of the golden chain, and that it was sharp enough both to pierce the hide of the monster and to cut out a slanderous tongue.

Criticism of the Paraphrase.

The extract gives a good idea of the author's sins of omission and commission. It will be seen, for example, that the tone of the entire passage is altered. The bit of repartee in the last sentence is wholly foreign to the Beowulf manner, which is outright and downright—the

---

[1] A prize offered by King Hygelak for the victor in the match.

very opposite of subtilty. The false manner is evident at once when we compare the reply of the hero in the original, 'Thou art the murderer of thine own brethren, and thou shalt be damned in Hell. Wait till to-night, and thou shalt see which of us is the stronger.'

The story is, if possible, more garbled than the style. The mission of the minstrel and the mangled account of the swimming-match have no essential or artistic relation to the context. They are merely inserted to add to the action of the piece.

The popularity of the book is attested by the number of editions through which it has passed. The volume contains also paraphrases of the legends about Arthur, Charlemagne, and Tannhäuser, as well as the story of the Nibelungs. These must account for its enduring success; but it is unfortunate that this, the poorest of the Beowulf paraphrases, should thus have found an audience which it did not deserve and could never have commanded for itself.

THERESE DAHN'S PARAPHRASE

Walhall. Germanische Götter- und Heldensagen. Für Alt und Jung am deutschen Herd erzählt von Felix Dahn und Therese Dahn, geb. Freiin von Droste-Hülshoff. Mit neunundfünfzig Bildertafeln, Textbildern, Kopfleisten und Schlussstücken nach Federzeichnungen von Johannes Gehrts. Kreuznach, Verlag von R. Voigtländer, 1883.

Seventh Edition, 1885.

Eleventh Edition, 1891.

Twelfth Edition (Leipzig), 1898.

8º, *Beowulf* (by Therese Dahn [1]), pp. 361–405, with two illustrations.

A Paraphrase in German Prose for General Readers.

[1] See p. 662.

Therese Dahn.

Therese Dahn, born Freiin von Droste-Hülshoff, was born in 1845, and married Felix Dahn in 1873. With him she published in 1873 at Leipzig a volume of poems (*Gedichte*). For certain of her verses in this volume she received high praise. She has since continued creative work. She resides at Breslau, where Felix Dahn is professor in the University. Of the stories in the present volume she wrote, beside *Beowulf, Die Wölsungen, Kudrun,* the story of König Wilkinus, &c., *Wieland der Schmied, Walther und Hildgund,* and the stories from the *Dietrich* saga and the *Nibelungen* saga.

Nature of the Paraphrase.

The following parts of the story are omitted entirely : the account of the first King Beowulf in the Prolog ; the Sigemund episode, Hrothgar's Discourse ; the Thrytho episode ; the Freawaru episode ; Beowulf's account of his Fight with Grendel as told to King Hygelac ; the Battle of Ravenswood.

Other changes in the story are as follows : the sorrows of the Danes as told in the Prolog are attributed to the reign of King Heremod ; in a separate Kapitel (III) are gathered the Sorrows of King Hrethel, the account of Ongentheow, the Fall of Hygelac, and the Death of Heardred. The Fight at Finnsburg is added and an original beginning provided for it.

Obscure words, phrases, and lines are omitted ; and explanatory words are inserted from time to time.

Indebtedness to Simrock.

The translation was evidently made with Simrock's translation [1] in hand ; possibly it may have been made directly

---

[1] See supra, p. 59.

from that version. Evidence of the dependence upon
Simrock may be found at every step. The forms of the
proper names invented by Simrock are repeated here
(e. g., Aeskhere, Hädkynn, Ochthere). His renderings of
the unique words in the poem (sometimes in a slightly
simplified form) are used in the paraphrase. Often the
original word used by Simrock is added in parentheses
(cf., e. g., Simrock, p. 72.6 with Dahn, p. 382, and p. 73.44
with Dahn, p. 383). Further evidence may be found by
comparing the extracts given in this work.

EXTRACT.

Hunferd, des Königs erster Sänger, hub da ein Streitlied an ; ihm
war Beowulfs Ankunft leid : denn er liebte es nicht, dass ein ihn anderer
an Ruhm übertreffe.

' Bist du der Beowulf, der einst im Wettkampf mit *Breka* durch die
See schwamm ? Wo ihr tollkühn in vermessenem Mut euer Leben in
den tiefen Wassern wagtet ? Weder Freund noch Feind konnten euch
abhalten. Da rudertet ihr in den Sund, masset die Meeresstrassen,
schlugt die Wasser mit den Händen, über die Tiefen gleitend. Die
winterkalte See stürmte und brauste : sieben Nächte schwammt ihr im
Wasser. Breka besiegte dich : er hatte mehr Kraft. Die Hochflut
warf ihn am nächsten Morgen ans Land, von wo er in seine Heimat
eilte, in das Land der *Brondinge*, wo er über Burg und Volk gebietet.'—
Page 370.

Criticism of the Paraphrase.

In many places the work is practically a translation, so
closely has the original been followed. The style is
agreeable and simple ; but most of what is beautiful in the
diction belongs to Simrock rather than to Frau Dahn.

The omissions are the most sensible that I have found
in a paraphrase. Nothing of first importance has been
lost.

STOPFORD BROOKE'S SELECTIONS

The History of Early English Literature, being the
History of English Poetry from its Beginnings to the
Accession of King Ælfred. By Stopford A. Brooke. New
York and London: The Macmillan Co., 1892.   8°, *Beowulf*,
pp. 12–92.
English Literature from the Beginning to the Norman
Conquest. By Stopford A. Brooke. New York and
London: The Macmillan Co., 1898. 8°, *Beowulf*, pp.
58–83.

Digest, Running Comment, and Translation of Copious
Extracts into Imitative Measures.

Reasons for including this Book.

This volume is included here because of the great influence it has had in forming popular notions regarding
the *Beowulf*. The eminence of Mr. Brooke as a critic and
as a poet has given him the attention of an audience
hardly commanded by any other writer included in this
paper.

Again, the number of lines actually translated by Mr.
Brooke is equal to that in many of the volumes described
in this section.

Difference between the two Editions.

The account in the second volume is much shorter than
that in the first; only twelve pages are given to the story
of Beowulf, while the first volume gives forty-three. The
later book omits all discussion of the episodes, and, although
parts of the older volume are retained, the matter is,
in general, re-written.

Method of Translation.

Translated extracts accompany the story as told by Mr. Brooke.

In his Preface (p. ix), the author speaks of the futility of prose translations of poetry, and of the inadequacy of modern English media for translating the spirit of the poetry. Finally he adopts a line which he hopes will 'fulfil the needs and follow closely the peculiarities' of Old English.

'I chose after many experiments, the trochaic movement used in this book, each half-line consisting of trochees following one another, with a syllable at the end, chiefly a long one, to mark the division of the line. I varied the line as much as I could, introducing, often rashly, metrical changes; for the fault of this movement is its monotony. I have sometimes tried an iambic movement, but rarely; for this trochaic line with a beat at the end of each half-verse seemed to me to get the nearest to the sound of the Anglo-Saxon line, even though it is frequently un-similar to that line itself. I used alliteration whenever I could, and stressed as much as possible the alliterated words, and I changed the length of the line with the changes of the original. But when I could not easily alliterate my line or stress the alliterated word, I did not try to do so.'

The author adopts an archaic diction. The word-order of the Old English is followed whenever possible.

Text Used.

The text appears to be that of Grein-Wülker (1883).

EXTRACT [1].

There at haven stood,   hung with rings the ship,
Ice-bright, for the outpath eager,   craft of Aethelings.
So their lord, the well-beloved,   all at length they laid
In the bosom of the bark,   him the bracelet-giver,—
By the mast the mighty king.   Many gifts were there
Fretted things of fairness   brought from far-off ways.—

[1] The swimming-match is not available for illustration here.

```
Never heard I of a keel      hung more comelily about
With the weeds of war,       with the weapons of the battle,
With the bills and byrnies.     On his breast there lay
A great heap of gems      that should go with him,
Far to fare away      in the Flood's possession¹.—Page 26.
```

Criticism of the Translation.

While the extracts cannot always be praised for their accuracy, they are, perhaps, sufficiently faithful for a popular work. When the author undertakes to emend the text for himself, or offers an original interpretation, his work is not always trustworthy. Emendations in his Beowulf selections, however, are rare.

The style of the extracts seems needlessly obscure. This is due in part to following too closely the original word-order (see lines 4 and 5 of the extract), and in part to the free use of archaic language. Mr. Brooke does not hesitate to employ such forms as, 'house-carles,' 'grit-wall,' 'ness-slopes,' 'host-shafts,' 'war-wood,' 'gold-flakèd shields,' 'grinning-masked helms,' which it would seem must be quite unintelligible to the majority of Mr. Brooke's readers.

The verse, which has been fully discussed above, is, perhaps, the most satisfactory feature of Mr. Brooke's work. Of course it is not strictly imitative, as he himself explains, but it gives a fairly good impression of the movement of the Old English verse.

¹ In the second edition, the penultimate line reads, 'Jewels great and heaped,' &c.

MISS RAGOZIN'S PARAPHRASE

Tales of the Heroic Ages. Siegfried, the Hero of the North, and Beowulf, the Hero of the Anglo-Saxons, by Zenaïde A. Ragozin. G. P. Putnam's Sons, New York and London, 1898. 8°, *Beowulf*, pp. 211–322, with Note at p. 323, and with four illustrations by George T. Tobin. School Edition, New York, W. B. Harison, 1900.

A Paraphrase in English Prose.

The Author, and the Aim of her Book.

Miss Zenaïde Alexeievna Ragozin, a Russian by birth, an American by adoption, has devoted herself to the popularization of history and mythology. In the series *Stories of the Nations*, she has published, *The Story of Chaldea, The Story of Assyria, The Story of Media, Babylon, and Persia, The Story of Vedic India.*' Of late she has turned her attention to the mythology of the various European nations, and has written of Siegfried, Frithjof, and Roland.

The object of her work may be given in her own words:—

' (The series is) intended as parallel reading to history, and planned to illustrate history. . . . Great changes are coming over the schools, . . . changes in the right direction, which may shortly amount to a revolution, when there will be no reason why these *Tales of the Heroic Ages* should not, although addressed to young people at large, find a place, if not in the school curriculum, at least in the wide margin of so-called 'Supplementary Reading.' May they prove acceptable, not alone to the young, to whom they are specially addressed, but also, as has been felicitously said, to "the old with young tastes." '—Pages xx, xxii.

Method of Paraphrase.

'(The style) should be simple and epical ; faithfully following the main lines, bringing out also the characteristic details—the poetical beauties, picturesque traits, and original dialogue, as much as may be consistent with necessary condensation and, frequently, elimination. It should be a consecutive, lively narrative, with the necessary elucidating explanations incorporated in the text and with the fewest and briefest possible footnotes, while it should contain no critical or mythological digressions. . . . What we want in telling it to the young, is to take the epic just as it is, condensing and expurgating, but not changing ; rendering the characters, scenes and situations with the faithfulness and reverence due to the masterpiece of a race ; using as much as possible, especially in the dialogue, the words of the original. . . . (The language) should be simple, though not untinged with quaintness, and even in places a certain degree of archaism.'— Pages xvi, xix, xxi.

Indebtedness to Earle.

'Professor Earle's[1] version has been fully utilized in the present volume, even to the extent of frequently making use of its wording, where it is not too archaic or literal for ordinary purposes.'—Page 330, footnote.

Some notion of the extent of this borrowing may be had by examining the extract printed below and the criticism that follows.

EXTRACT.

Yet there was one eye that gleamed not with merriment and goodwill, one head that hatched no friendly thoughts, because the heart swelled with malice and envy. Unferth it was, the king's own story-teller, who sat at his feet, to be ready at all times to amuse him. He broached a quarrelsome theme—an adventure in Beowulf's youth, the only contest in his record the issue of which, though hard fought, might be called doubtful. For this Unferth was an envious wight, whose soul grudged that any man should achieve greater things than himself.

'Art thou not,' he began tauntingly, 'that same Beowulf who strove with Breca on open sea in a swimming-match, in which ye both

[1] See supra, p. 91.

wantonly exposed your lives, and no man, either friend or foe, could
turn you from the foolish venture? A se'nnight ye twain toiled in
the realm of the waters, and, if I err not, he outdid thee in swimming,
for he had greater strength. Wherefore I fear me much that thou
mayest meet with sorry luck if thou darest to bide here for Grendel
for the space of a whole night.'

Criticism of the Paraphrase.

It may be inferred from the dependence upon the work
of Earle that Miss Ragozin's knowledge of Old English
is of the slightest. This inference is borne out by frequent
misapprehension of the original sense, due in large measure
to the use of a single translation. Thus on page 245,
Grendel is called 'the God-sent scourge,' and, again, on
p. 322, Beowulf is described as having been 'most genial
to his nobles.' Both of these errors are due to misapprehension of Professor Earle's translation. The list
of proper names on p. 331 reveals an ignorance of some
fundamental facts of Old English pronunciation. Of course,
an intimate knowledge of the Beowulf style and diction
is not indispensable to the writer of a paraphrase, but the
writer who has it will naturally be superior to the writer
without it. For illustration, Miss Thomson[1] never mis-
interprets a passage as does Miss Ragozin on page 264,
where nearly every sentence is false to the Beowulf
manner.

The paraphrase is slightly disfigured by the distinctively
Romance words which disfigure Earle's translation.

But these slight defects need not blind us to the service
done by Miss Ragozin in making Beowulf accessible to
school children. The style is, in general, strong and
effective, not without some of the beauty and dignity of
the Old English, but relieved of the more obscure and
recondite features of that style.

[1] See infra, p. 143.

MR. CHURCH'S PARAPHRASE

Heroes of Chivalry and Romance. By the Rev. A. J. Church, M.A. London: Seeley and Company, 1898. 8°, *Beowulf*, pp. 3–60. With two illustrations in colours by George Morrow.

Beowulf Retold.

Contents of the Volume.

'The Story of Beowulf,' 'King Arthur and the Round Table,' 'The Treasure of the Nibelungs.'

Indebtedness to Kemble and Earle.

'In writing the story of Beowulf I have been helped by Kemble's translation and notes [1], and still more by Professor Earle's [2] admirable edition.'—Author's Note.

Nature of the Paraphrase.

All obscure words (especially kennings) and lines are dropped. Many explanatory remarks are inserted to elucidate the story. All speeches are greatly shortened. Beowulf's tale of the fight is omitted entirely. The episodes are omitted, with the exception of the Sigemund episode, one-half of which is translated into heroic couplets, and the Finn episode, which is referred to in a single stanza which paraphrases the story.

Concerning the Author.

The Rev. Alfred John Church (born 1829) is known chiefly for his popularizations of the classics. His best-known works are *Stories from Homer* and *Stories from Virgil*.

[1] See supra, p. 33.   [2] See supra, p. 91.

The present volume is an attempt to do for some of the
Germanic legends what had already been done for Homer
and Virgil.

EXTRACT.

But while they feasted envy stirred in the heart of Unferth, son
of Ecglaf. He was the King's orator, and he took it ill that Beowulf
should have come to the land of the Danes on this great enterprise,
for he was one who could not endure that any man under heaven
should do greater deeds than himself. Therefore he stood up in
the hall and spake: 'Art thou that Beowulf who contended with
Breca in swimming on the open sea? 'Twas, indeed, a foolhardy
thing so to put your lives in jeopardy, yet no man could turn you
from your adventure. Seven days and nights ye toiled, one against
the other, but he in the end prevailed, for he had the greater
strength. And on the eighth morning the waves cast him ashore
on the land of the Heathoram, whence he journeyed back to the
city of the Bronding, of which he was lord. So did Breca, son of
Beanstan, make good his boast against thee.'

Criticism of the Paraphrase.

The extract is so much fuller than the other parts of the
paraphrase that it hardly gives a fair notion of the nature
of the work. The author has appreciated the dramatic
quality of the swimming episode and preserved it nearly
entire. Other parts of the story are much less fortunate.

A little knowledge of Old English would have done the
author no harm, and would have saved him from some
errors. His most evident mistakes are in the forms of the
proper names. Such forms as these occur in his book:
Veleda, Hugon, Weopstan (sic), Hrethin, Hrethet.

The diction is unfortunate. The coast-warden becomes
a 'squire' (p. 7); Heorot is a 'banqueting hall' (p. 4,
showing the influence of Kemble's translation); Beowulf
and Breca were 'pages at the King's court' (p. 13, showing
the influence of Earle's translation).

Petty inaccuracies occur throughout, such as, 'I counsel

that thou refuse not' (p. 9); 'A faithful squire must needs know the troubles of his lord' (p. 7). In point of accuracy this version is quite inferior to the work of Miss Thomson[1]; and in point of style and atmosphere to that of Mr. Jones[2], Miss Ragozin[3], or Miss Thomson. The book, however, is readable, and the author's name will doubtless serve to give it a certain success.

MISS THOMSON'S PARAPHRASE

The Adventures of Beowulf, translated from the Old English and adapted to the Use of Schools by Clara Thomson[4]. London: Horace Marshall and Son, 1899. 8°, pp. 95. In the 'New English Series,' edited by E. E. Speight.

A Paraphrase in English Prose.

Aim of the Volume.

' It is meant mainly to arouse in children an interest in the beginnings of our literature—a subject that is still terribly neglected in schools. It makes no pretension to being an adequate or satisfactory version for grown-up readers.'—Page 6.

Method of Paraphrase.

'[Discrepancies in the poem] I have endeavoured to smooth over by omission or by very slight additions ; and whenever of two readings of a doubtful passage, one is more easily comprehensible than the other, I have always adhered to this, even if on philological grounds it seems less probable.' . . .

---

[1] See infra, p. 143.   [2] See supra, p. 123.
[3] See supra, p. 138.
[4] Miss Thomson is better known as the biographer of Samuel Richardson. See *Samuel Richardson, a Biographical and Critical Study.* London, 1900.

'Many of the episodes in the story have been greatly shortened or altogether omitted, since they interrupt the course of the narrative, or divert the interest from the main theme.'—Pages 5, 6.

This statement is more modest than need be. It will be found that only two of the episodes are passed without mention—the Prolog and the Tale of Thrytho. The Legend of Sigemund and the Tale of Finn are rather fully treated, and the Story of Freawaru and the Battle of Ravenswood are both referred to. In each case the episodes are carefully woven into the story, and that without superfluous words.

The words and sentences which are supplied are very carefully chosen, and most of them have a prototype somewhere in the poem.

EXTRACT.

Now, though most of Hrothgar's men rejoiced to see Beowulf, and honoured him for his generous thought in coming to their help, there was one who looked on him with dislike and envy, and was jealous of the favour shown him by the king. This was Hunferth, who was sitting on the daïs at Hrothgar's feet. And when he heard what this visitor intended to do, he grew angry and moody, because he could not bear that any other man on earth should obtain greater honour than he himself. So he began to rake up old tales that he had heard of Beowulf, and tried to turn them to his hurt, saying scornfully—

'Art thou that Beowulf who once strove on the wide sea in a swimming-match with Breca, when ye two in boasting dared to breast the wave, and for vainglory risked your lives in the deep water? There was no man, friend nor foe, who could dissuade you from that sorrowful journey; but ye swam in the surf, stretching out your arms over the waves, and stirring up the surge with your hands. So did ye glide across the ocean, while the waves weltered in wintry storms, and for seven nights ye laboured in the tumult of the seas. But in the end the victory was with Breca, for his might was the greater. Then on the morning of the eighth day the tide bore him to the shore of Norway, whence he visited his beloved home, the fair city of safety, where he ruled over many people, over towns and treasure. Truly he did perform all his boast against thee.'

Criticism of the Paraphrase.

In the opinion of the present writer, no better paraphrase of *Beowulf* exists.

It is perhaps unfortunate that the word 'translated' is used on the title-page, for this is misleading. The proper form is that used on the cover of the book, 'Beowulf, told by Miss Clara Thomson.'

It were sufficient praise to point out that the author has contrived to retain practically all of the poem, without ever falsifying its spirit by introducing a superabundance of explanatory phrases[1]. She is always true to the story (as Miss Ragozin[2] is not, for example, in the first section of her work); she is equally true to the spirit of the poem (as Mr. Gibb[3] is not). The style is both vigorous and simple, not unworthy of the story it tells.

It will be surprising if Miss Thomson's work is not popular in England, and the book should be known and used in this country.

---

[1] The author's argument against inserting the Prolog is sound enough; but the omission of any part of the poem in a paraphrase so good as Miss Thomson's is to be regretted.

[2] See supra, p. 138.　　　　　　　[3] See supra, p. 128.

K

APPENDIX II

A BIBLIOGRAPHY OF WORKS WHICH CONTAIN SELECTIONS FROM BEOWULF TRANSLATED INTO ENGLISH

(Only works which translate at least thirty lines are noted.)

TEN BRINK, BERNHARD, AND KENNEDY, HORACE, in Early English Literature (to Wiclif). London and New York, 1883. Verse.

BROWN, ANNA R., in Poet Lore, II, 133, 185. Verse, ll. 26–53, and 1493–1571.

GUMMERE, F. B., in the American Journal of Philology, VII, 77, ll. 1–52. Verse.

—— in Germanic Origins (New York, 1892), pp. 109 ff. Verse.

LONGFELLOW, HENRY WADSWORTH, in Poets and Poetry of Europe, lines 18–40; 53–83; 189–257; 1789–1803; 2455–2462. Verse.

MORLEY, HENRY, in English Writers, I, pp. 287 ff. (second edition, London, 1887). Verse.

ROBINSON, W. CLARKE, in Introduction to our Early English Literature (London, 1885). Lines 87–98 (verse), and 1–52 (prose).

SMITH, C. SPRAGUE, in the New Englander, IV, p. 49. Lines 711–838; Section XII, Section XIII, 1493–1652; Section XXIII, Section XXIV. Verse.

SWEET, HENRY, in Warton's History of English Poetry, ed. W. Carew Hazlitt (London, 1877). Vol. II, pp. 11–12. Prose.

TOLMAN, A. H., in Transactions of the Modern Language Association, III, pp. 19 ff. In the 'Style of Anglo-Saxon Poetry.' Prose.

Incomplete Paraphrase.

PALMER, BERTHA, in Stories from the Classic Literature of many Nations (New York, 1898), pp. 262–263. Beowulf's Fight with Grendel, using J. L. Hall's translation as a basis.

APPENDIX III

TWO WORKS NAMED 'BEOWULF'

I.

Beowulf, Roman von Karl Manno (pseud. Carl von Lemcke). In *Deutsche Roman-Zeitung*, Jahrg. 19, Bde. 1, 2. Berlin, 1882.

A modern romance, having no relation to the Old English poem.

II.

Mr. S. H. Church's 'Beowulf.'

Beowulf, a Poem by Samuel Harden Church. New York: Stokes and Co., 1901.

An original poem, using some of the Beowulf material.

After speaking of his original intention of translating the *Beowulf*, which he later discarded, the author says:—

'I have . . . composed an original narrative in which the leading characters and some of the incidents of the early work[1] have been freely used, but as materials only. I have transferred to my hero, Beowulf, the picturesque history of Sceaf[2]; have changed the relationship of characters and incidents; have inserted the illumination of Beowulf's soul, and his banishment; and have introduced the love motive between Beowulf and Freaware that runs through the poem to the end. Indeed the structure, language, style, description, elaboration, interpretation, and development of the story are new. I have arbitrarily laid the scene in England, under purely idealized conditions; and have initiated nearly all that the poem contains of womanhood, of love, of religion, of state-policy, and of domestic life and manners. It is clear, therefore, that my work must not be judged either as a translation, version, or paraphrase of the old Beowulf.'

[1] i. e., the translation.   [2] Scyld

INDEX OF TRANSLATORS